WILDSCAPE

"By exploring how animals, insects, and birds use their five senses to find food or a mate, and to communicate and defend themselves, Lawson eloquently illustrates that we also need to use our five senses to connect with the natural world. And we do not have to go far to experience biodiversity: it's right outside our front door. What is required is our willingness to unplug, listen, observe, touch, smell, and reconnect with the wonders of nature."

—HEATHER HOLM,
pollinator conservationist and author

"By taking us deep into the lives of backyard creatures, Lawson takes us out of our solipsism and grants us the gift of swapping stories with butterflies, chipmunks, and beetles. As we get to know these other cultures and sense the world through our shared experiences, we travel deeper into our landscapes and squash biases instead of bugs. With incredible tidbits of science and story (boy, is poop useful), this book asks us to live a wilder, more willful life that honors the intricate relationships right beneath our noses."

—BENJAMIN VOGT,
author of *A New Garden Ethic* and *Prairie Up*

"*Wildscape* is a book that brings us closer to the world around us. Rarely do we find storytellers capable of sharing personal observations alongside cutting-edge research. Nancy Lawson reconnects readers to the wondrous dynamics among plants and animals."

—REBECCA McMACKIN,
ecological horticulturist and designer

Wildscape

Trilling CHIPMUNKS,
Beckoning BLOOMS,
Salty BUTTERFLIES,
and other
SENSORY WONDERS
of NATURE

NANCY LAWSON

PA PRESS

PRINCETON ARCHITECTURAL PRESS · NEW YORK

Published by
Princeton Architectural Press
A division of Chronicle Books LLC
70 West 36th Street
New York, New York 10018
papress.com

Printed and bound in China
26 25 24 23   4 3 2 1 First edition

ISBN: 978-1-7972-2247-9

Editor: Sara Stemen
Designer: Benjamin English

Library of Congress Cataloging-in-Publication Data
available upon request

Contents

A few years ago, a writer for a men's magazine called me for help. He was putting together a fun piece on activities for fathers and sons, and he wanted to include ideas for nurturing nature at home. The information had to be manly enough for his editors, he cautioned, and planting for butterflies wouldn't cut it.

As I struggled to divide the natural world along stereotypical gender lines, I ticked off a few tips for projects that would be interesting, life-giving, and even helpful to butterflies, whether these hypermasculine magazine readers knew it or not. They could plant a bat garden with night-blooming flowers that feed moths. They could build a brush pile for snakes, frogs, birds, and turtles. They could make a mini meadow for fireflies and caterpillars.

We talked for forty-five minutes, but there was one thing I forgot. "Did you tell them about all the cool animals we see having sex in the yard?" my husband, Will, asked when he got home that night. Somehow, our wildlife peep shows had escaped my memory, and

To yucca moths, a single plant represents the entire universe. Caterpillars eat seeds, adults mate on flowers, and pupae overwinter in the soil below. Likewise, yucca plants (shown also on previous spread) can't live without yucca moths, their only pollinators.

maybe that's why my tips didn't make it into the article—a good thing, in retrospect, given how the editors chose to frame the story. "Be a Backyard Badass," the headline screamed, and most of the piece was about humans going on the attack, with a subhead encouraging readers to blast rockets, fend off wild animals, and "raise a ruckus." A section on the next page titled "Suburban Warfare" advised the audience to "tame backyard terrorists," from aphids to raccoons to mountain lions.

The single-minded editors didn't just bury the lede; they missed it altogether. Your backyard—or deck or balcony or neighborhood green space—is sometimes a battleground; that much is true. But it's not *your* battleground—or at least, it shouldn't be. When you treat it respectfully, here's what it could be: a place of endless growth and decay, birth and death, love and war, sweetness and light, lies and deceit and subterfuge. An epic tale of ancient cultures and storied family lines going back thousands of years. A safe haven of leaves and logs and snags for mothers and fathers raising their kids. A singles bar of ponds and perches for the lovelorn. A doctor's office of chemically fortified plants for the sick and wounded. A grocery store and a mixed-unit housing development of trees and shrubs and flowers for a diverse community of pollinators, predators, prey, decomposers, and other workers essential to a bustling economy.

Your outdoor surroundings are a vibrant universe, a place where many languages are spoken, sometimes in sensory alphabets we humans have hardly even begun to decipher. It's swirling with hidden messages: ephemeral molecules spelling out an invitation or piecing together a cry for help. Ultrasound clicks you can't hear and ultraviolet colors you can't see. Calls of alarm, distress, defense, and companionship that reach your ears but require a translator to decode.

If you treat the local environment like the homeland it's meant to be, you'll be exposed to more cultures and ideas and ways of life than if you visited with people from every country in the world. Butterflies will land on your toes, and fireflies will court on your knees. You'll cross paths with beetles who spend months raising their children, living together as families long after their young have hatched. You'll see hummingbirds make extraordinary swooping flights to impress their beloveds and mourning doves building their nests together. You'll watch a fox eating tidbits from the grass in the early morning sunlight and feel a rabbit hop over your shoe as the evening settles in. You'll hear the anthems of frogs and bluebirds declaring the spring season, and you'll sit among hooting owls and shooting stars closing out the year in December.

You'll see that your yard and your community green spaces are not really yours at all, but the gathering place of countless sovereign nations, a refuge for the increasingly displaced. Faced with the blare and glare of extraneous human interference, many would-be habitats are stunted before they ever really get off the ground. Noise pollution, light pollution, lawns, and other negative by-products of superficial human progress are disrupting the connections among flora and fauna as well as our own ability to connect with the nature in our communities. But your space can be different, once you stop trying so hard to defend its borders and start looking at the world from the perspectives of other beings who live there.

Many books have been written about gardening for human senses, but our own sensory experiences are impoverished if we don't take the time to consider the sensory ecology of other species. Worse, the societal premium we place on our dominant sense—vision—leads us to suppress the habitats that animals and plants require. One of the many tragedies of the modern era is that the spaces where we live and work and play have been shoehorned into conformity, designed to be uniform and boring and flat for the sake of convenience and profit. What a great loss that is to us as participants in this world—in every sense: aesthetically, tactilely, aurally, olfactorily, and gustatorily. And what an even greater loss to all the other creatures who could thrive in more varied landscapes.

To understand their needs and how we're hindering their ability to survive, I started by trying to learn everything I could about my wild

This may look like your average insect tryst, but the story of blister beetles (told on page 136) is full of intrigue, involving thievery, weaponry, false identity, and fatal deception.

neighbors in my own habitat in Maryland. And when the pandemic hit, I never really left. I couldn't interview the plants and animals about their experiences, so I hit the books, read studies, and turned to nature's human interpreters. Sometimes I found the answers quickly. Other times my questions led to more questions. One inquiry even resulted in a collaboration with two overseas scientists. More often than not, I couldn't get exact answers about the behaviors or traits I was witnessing, but I could get approximate ones: best guesses based on knowledge of similar interactions among related species.

While in the process of reading hundreds of papers, interviewing dozens of scientists, and immersing myself in my habitat, I also tried honing my own senses. Like many Americans, I have poor eyesight. I also have only half my hearing. But those obstacles pale in comparison with the electronic and gas-powered distractions and noise humans create, the false urgencies and expectations we adhere to. Many animals are specialized in their needs, but we are universal in our destruction. Our life spans are short, and our attention spans are even shorter. Our culture values "living in the moment," but we've turned every moment into an exclamation point. Humans once planned their monuments for decades, sometimes centuries, in advance. They knew they'd never live to see the ripe fruits of their labors, just as they'd never live as long as the trees around them. Now we can build a house in a few weeks; stock it with furniture and toilet paper made from old-growth forests; sit inside, losing our long-distance vision in front of computer screens; and pay landscape crews to go deaf as they obliterate the outdoors.

When I started writing this book, the pandemic slowed down time. Then my father died, and I forgot what year it was for a while. I went from a sapling to a tree with more rings at my core, feeling the rain on my newly exposed roots as the ground eroded around me. But the roots still went deep, and the animals were still busy, keeping me company and planting new seeds in the shadows of my grief. Some appear here as recurring characters, competing with Will for my affections: Mr. Chippie and my green-frog boyfriend, the sassy wrens and hummingbirds. Other friendships, like those I made with a glamorous pink planthopper and the camouflaged looper caterpillars, were more fleeting. But they all took me on fascinating journeys, offering tiny windows into their sensory worlds.

Mark Twain famously said, "Travel is fatal to prejudice, bigotry, and narrow-mindedness.... Broad, wholesome, charitable views of men and things cannot be acquired by vegetating in one little corner of the earth all one's lifetime." A hundred fifty years later, I'm not sure I agree. Aside from the aspersions he casts on plants—what's so bad about vegetating?—we now live in a time when many people don't even know their human neighbors, much less their wild ones. Studies show that being around nature makes us smarter, happier, and kinder. Exploring in your own backyard can open up your imagination, and in the process, your humanity. I hope this book serves as inspiration for creating your own travel guide to your patch of the planet—and your own handbook of etiquette for respecting the many cultures crossing in and out of your borders every day.

CHAPTER 1

The Scentscape

The answer, my friend, is blowin' in the wind.
—Bob Dylan

Their teasing shadows come into view first, flickering apparitions at the edges of my current known world: *now you see us, now you don't.* They cross the street and circle back, flying over kids who ride by and belt out songs about evil viruses, over adults who share tips from a safe distance about where to get toilet paper and bread, over me as I transplant asters and check my phone to see the latest update: the governor has issued a stay-at-home order to try to stem the tide of rising COVID-19 cases.

As the male butterflies circle closer to their love interests and send pheromones into the breeze—using both visual and olfactory cues to advertise their virility, their territory, their readiness for love—I walk beneath them to retrieve some messages of my own. In the mailbox are four postcards advising me to "battle back" against nature. Beneath a dreamily fake, Photoshopped scene of toddlers admiring a blue butterfly seen only in the tropics, a local lawn and pest control company proclaims: "Kids love butterflies, not ticks or mosquitoes."

A question mark butterfly surveys his territory. Male butterflies of many species search visually for mates and release pheromones as they fly closer.

Virginia creeper makes a perfect nesting spot. Many animals find visual and olfactory cover under plants.

The fifth piece of mail is addressed in a child's careful script, containing a letter sent from a thousand miles away:

Dear Ms. Lawson,

My name is Brice. I am a twelve year old boy. I live on Longboat Key in Florida. I love wildlife and gardening. I have been using native plants more and more lately because of their benefits to wildlife and the ecosystem. After reading your book, *The Humane Gardener*, I have decided to use nearly all natives and start collecting tree branches when people throw them out to pile in our backyard for wildlife. I also just convinced my mom to let me grow a patch of Virginia Creeper which I had been ruthlessly killing for years just because it is a *little* exuberant. Thank you for including Spanish Needle in your book. I have let it overrun a lot of our yard and from the time the bees come out in the morning till the sun goes down I have yet to see less than ten bees of all kinds flying happily around the Spanish Needle at any given time. It also attracts tons of butterflies. Yet I have never seen it mentioned in any other book even books of plants for wildlife as much more than a "weed." Thank you also for acknowledging the importance of slugs and other native insects commonly known as "pests" and that they have as much right to live as any other animals.

Yours sincerely,
Brice

I settle into the wooden chair under our maple tree, hoping to be still long enough to get more than a fleeting view of spring's evanescent spirits. For hours, the butterflies chase each other, occasionally

This spring scene may look serene, but the very air above the garden in front of our house is filled with hidden messages that only plants and animals can decipher.

offering a quick peek of their brilliant orange inner wings. They land near the sap still oozing from the sickly elm we nurture just for them, the one whose bark they hide in each winter and whose sugars they drink each spring. They fly to the stepping-stones, to the logs lining the pathways, and to the bits of dead grasses I've pulled and left in piles for birds to use as nesting material. They spread their sun-soaked wings and beckon me to find my camera, even though I know that by the time I come back, they'll be up in the air again, floating above us and the earthly messes we've made.

The airspace around our home swirls with the energy of countless beings who make their lives alongside us. Mingling in the warming breezes are volatile molecules that launch love affairs, start wars, and issue dire news alerts, fake and otherwise, among friends and foes alike. Some scents are ephemeral, while others, especially those of mammals, are longer lasting. Though largely hidden from us—I'd never know the fox was lifting his leg over the pedestal of the birdbath every night if I hadn't seen it on the wildlife camera—olfactory cues can be harder for animals to conceal from one another than visual or auditory behaviors. They can also regulate the activities of entire communities; the fox's wanderings likely even influence where birds choose to nest and rabbits run for cover.

A strong wind comes through, and one butterfly waits it out at the tip of an elm branch. He holds tight long enough to reveal his identity: a question mark (a species named for the white punctuation-like coloration on his brown outer wings). With wings closed, he looks like a leaf, a disguise accentuated by the complex curves that define his shape. Known as crypsis, this visual trickery helps question marks and a related species, Eastern commas, to elude birds, spiders, and other predators.

I wish it could also protect them from the mosquito-spraying companies that fill mailboxes across my community with their harmful propaganda. Industry claims of targeted spraying aren't based in reality; droplets of poison spread far and wide. Over the past several years, mass die-offs of monarch butterflies immediately after mosquito spraying have been reported in at least two US states, Maryland and Nebraska. No insects are safe from insecticide diffusing through the air or coating the leaves they land on and eat.

As I fold Brice's letter, a question mark lands near me and unfolds her wings. She's had a long day. Maybe she's already laid her eggs on the hackberries or false nettles. These are the plants whose scents and visual cues she seeks for her young, tasting them with the chemoreceptors in her feet before finally laying eggs. They're the plants her caterpillars have evolved to eat. They're also some of the many that lawn and pest companies routinely cut and spray away. But in a little coastal town in Florida, there's at least one young person who's determined not to let them.

More Than Meets the Nose

The emerging field of aeroecology, a term coined just fifteen years ago, puts the airspace of the lower atmosphere on a par with the earthly domains occupied by more grounded organisms. It encompasses the olfactory realm and more, including the way sound travels and the effects of man-made hazards like buildings and drones on natural phenomena. Aeroecology takes into account changing atmospheric conditions as well as the influences of sunlight, moonlight, and geomagnetic and gravitational forces.

As naturally grounded beings, we're not primed to think about such an intangible and undefined place, yet it teems with life: dragonflies and butterflies migrating by the millions; woodcocks and hummingbirds swooping and swooning in elaborate aerial displays; and winds carrying pollen, spores, seeds, and invertebrates to altitudes of more than thirty miles. We might be surprised to learn that some bird species live aloft for months at a time without ever touching down. Or that shifting winds don't just affect which plants receive pollen directly but also alter flight paths of pollinators toward or away from flowers. It can be hard to imagine that what's happening in the airspace has ripple effects across the animal kingdom: that temperature and wind speed influence Texas moth migrations, for example, which in turn affect the feeding habits of their predators, Brazilian free-tailed bats, which can ultimately determine food supplies for the peregrine falcons and red-tailed hawks who hunt those bats.

"That a habitat could be invisible or is capable of being present one moment and gone the next is far outside most personal and professional experiences," wrote ecologist Robert Diehl and his colleagues, citing these examples and more in their case for protecting this unappreciated realm. In their US Geological Survey paper "Extending the Habitat Concept to the Airspace," they noted that the aerosphere has been almost completely ignored—and is increasingly harmed—because of our biased perspective of life on Earth.

Of all the sensory inputs experienced by our wild neighbors, their olfactory world may be the hardest to grasp, reliant as it is on ever-changing conditions that are largely amorphous. It's difficult enough to comprehend that the world is full of colors outside our visual spectrum and sounds too high or low for us to hear. But many odors are so fleeting and so malleable, constantly mixing together and dissipating, that understanding and describing their structures is even harder than catching sand in a cracking bucket; you might grab some bits momentarily but lose others, never fully quantifying how a given scent compound runs its course in the natural environment, let alone all the organisms catching its drift.

Our human olfactory systems are fairly useless in detecting unseen and unheard communications that aren't meant for an organism so "blind in the nose," as naturalist Craig Childs labels us in his book *The Animal Dialogues*. It's not that we lack smelling capacity; in fact, at the time of Childs's writing in 2007, scientists believed that we had the potential to detect only ten thousand odors, but research has since boosted that number to a trillion. The way we detect them, though, makes them harder for us to separate and name. While other senses send signals through the thalamus, a kind of gateway processing system in our brains, smells head more directly to the parts of our brains that control memory and emotion. As mammals, we can sense fear and anxiety through our scent receptors. Odors lure us to mates and warn us of spoiled food and impending calamity. But it's possible to lose our sense of smell and still survive. We even communicate fairly well sans scent: for better or worse, there was no Smell-O-Vision available on the socially distant Zoom interviews conducted for this book.

The dominance of sight and sound in humans can diminish our worldview—or our collective inhale—and has long impeded our insights (insmells?) into the inner lives of other species. It stymies our notion of what's possible: until fifty years ago, most scientific papers repeated the myth that only a handful of birds could smell. Frogs were thought to lack olfactory abilities too. Only recently have researchers begun to understand the social and scent-based dynamics of creatures like snakes, discovering that they too commune with friends, defend young, and babysit for one another.

"A lot of the reason that we didn't deem them capable of all these things is that we can't experience it: they are communicating in ways

We were lucky to spot this well-camouflaged garter snake moving along our woodchipped path. Male snakes would be able to locate her by sniffing out the methyl ketones in her skin; they can assess the body size and condition of females based on pheromone cues alone.

that we don't," says Melissa Amarello, who studies the social lives of snakes and leads Advocates for Snake Preservation in New Mexico. "Scent is everything to them. They can see, they can hear. But those chemical cues are how they're doing most of their talking and experiencing the world."

Lacking facial expressions, vocalizations, and limbs, snakes are inscrutable to a species that reads intention into every raised eyebrow or waving hand. Amarello is an exception who knows how to interpret their cues; she recalls the overwhelming, musty smell of fear at a rattlesnake roundup in Texas, where thousands of snakes were flushed out of dens with gasoline, tormented, and killed for entertainment. "If those were rabbits...it would be excruciating to experience because they would be screaming out loud and we could all hear it. We just can't hear it when snakes are doing it."

It takes empathy, but by using our imagination we can begin to understand how different organisms perceive the world through their noses and antennae and tongues and feet—and also how they spit it back out again, adding ever-greater layers of complexity to the already crowded scentscape.

Shooting the Poop: Avoiding Detection

Following my own often-stuffy nose into scent explorations usually starts with keeping my eyes open for breaks in the usual patterns of my garden, a routine that led me to my first epic scatological show. Though I'd handled the doody duty on more than one occasion at local nature festivals, explaining to toddlers the nuances of coyote and deer poop, getting all up in the backside business of our wild neighbors had long been at the bottom of my to-do list.

My five-decade-long streak of innocence about such indecorous matters came to a halt one September afternoon when I rounded a corner to water some seedlings and found an orange-and-black caterpillar resting on a log. Certain that this butterfly baby was the offspring of a mother variegated fritillary who'd laid eggs in front of me a few weeks before, I flattened myself at ground level to watch her through my macro lens.

Soon the caterpillar was booking it over to a nearby violet, where she chowed down heartily and offered a closeup view of a bulge moving along her body as she ate. It wasn't long before the remnants of the meal reached their natural conclusion, and what happened next was so fast and startling that I didn't trust my eyes. The caterpillar

Adult female variegated fritillary butterflies search for violets in our meadow garden in late summer.

While munching on a violet, a variegated fritillary caterpillar ejects green frass like a cannonball out of her backside.

Silver-spotted skipper caterpillars (above) also engage in projectile-pooping to avoid detection by predators like Northern paper wasps, who provision their nests with caterpillars.

raised her back end, pushed out a lime-green ball that hovered at the tip, and shot it like a cannon—or maybe she popped it like bubble gum or pulled it back in; it was so fast I couldn't decide. Was this some kind of caterpillar fart? Was she constipated? Had she aborted the mission, having not yet eaten enough leafy greens to fully hit the eject button?

Postsnack, my ravenous little friend went back onto the log to take a breather. I stepped away to refill the watering can, and by the time I returned, she was starting the cycle again: voracious eating, resting, and repeating. This time, my camera caught the projectile-pooping action, leaving little doubt as to the nature of the behavior—a phenomenon, I would soon learn, that has numerous names: frass flinging, poop shooting, turd tossing, fecal firing, and—when discussing micro-moth caterpillars, who use their tiny legs to throw frass more than twenty body lengths away—turd hurling and butt flicking.

The terminology lesson came courtesy of biology professor Martha Weiss, who noticed the mini ballistic missiles of butterfly larvae more than twenty years before I did, when she kept silver-spotted skipper caterpillars in plastic shoeboxes to study how they build leaf shelters. It was her ears that first alerted her to repeated "ping! ping! ping!" sounds while working in her lab at Georgetown University. Investigating further, Weiss saw pellets of frass—or caterpillar waste—ricocheting off the box's plastic walls. "Every once in a while I'd see a frass pellet flying through the air," she recalls. "And I thought, 'What the heck?'"

A call to a colleague and a subsequent literature survey unearthed a 1913 paper that included a drawing of an "anal comb," a kind of mechanical hatch that opens when a surge in hydrostatic pressure

An adult silver-spotted skipper perches on a sunflower. Males are known to chase away other insects from their territorial perches.

shoots poop out of a caterpillar's back end. Further searches for ecological explanations gleaned scant results, so Weiss tested a few theories herself: Were the caterpillars ejecting frass at such velocity to keep their shelters from getting crowded? Was frass removal important to their hygiene? Did it prevent natural enemies from finding them?

Through a series of ingenious experiments, she found strong support for the last hypothesis. Caterpillars forced to reside near frass were much more likely to be killed by predatory wasps homing in on the odors. Weiss's discovery highlighted the importance of what she calls "the other end" of foraging ecology. Significant effort is devoted to studying the causes and consequences of finding and eating food, but very little attention is paid to waste elimination because, as she notes, "Who wants to look at poop?"

There's a reason Weiss first observed frass flinging with her ears and I first learned about it with my eyes: our noses wouldn't detect it. In fact, the inoffensive nature of insect poop, particularly that of caterpillars and other plant eaters, is among Weiss's many convincing arguments for augmenting the still-nascent field of defecation ecology. "It smells like nothing," Weiss says. "It's just broken-up leaves."

It clearly smells like a lot more to many organisms. While some insects distance themselves from their own waste, Weiss describes others doing the opposite. Male bark beetles are housekeepers who haul away the poop of their mates from the nuptial chambers. Hawkmoth caterpillars smear their own feces all over themselves to prevent tachinid flies from laying eggs on their bodies (a nasty fate, given that the hatching fly larvae eat caterpillars alive); pyralid and choreutid moth larvae create fortresses of "fecal stalactites" around themselves on the undersides of leaves. One type of predatory assassin bug covers himself in a disguise made of wood and waste to sneak up on unsuspecting termites.

The inventive uses of insect poop appear limitless, but their main goals are universal: to issue chemical warning signals and to construct visual camouflage for predation and protection. For her part, my fritillary caterpillar wanted nothing to do with her own frass, ejecting it so far away that I couldn't find it. But if she was trying to distance herself for the same reason Weiss's silver-spotted skippers did, she may not have been entirely successful at warding off uninvited guests. Occasionally swinging her head toward her back end, as if wanting to bite it, she seemed irritated in a way that reminded me of when my dog used to lash out at gnats flying around her in the garden or whip her head back after passing gas.

Thrashing about, I would soon learn, is a common method used by caterpillars to fend off enemies. After I shared the video on Instagram, a naturalist friend spotted the source of her annoyance: a tiny, almost imperceptible parasitoid wasp was making his way up the last setae, or hairs, with the goal of laying eggs directly on or in the caterpillar's body. Not only that, but there may have even been a second wasp, a "hyperparasite" on top of the first one—an infinite hall of mirrors, nature repeating itself by eating, pooping it out, and taking it all back in again in a cycle of endless destruction and renewal.

If our little caterpillar was indeed successful in her clandestine mission to shoot her poop pellets far and wide, how did the parasitic wasps find their fleshy prey? It could have been the plants who gave her away.

When Plants Fight Back

Plants may look immobile to us, but the one caught in the mandibles of the fritillary caterpillar was no shrinking violet. Scent explorer Harold McGee pulls the human-centric notion of plants as passive players up by the roots, suggesting that we've got it backward: "Animals move because they're less autonomous than plants are," he writes in *Nose Dive: A Field Guide to the World's Smells*. "They can't feed and build themselves and spin out volatiles from just air and water and soil and sunlight, as plants astonishingly do."

Twitter has nothing on plants' mercurial broadcasts, odorous chemical compounds that mediate interactions with other organisms and convey an extraordinary amount of detail as they float across the landscape. Known as secondary metabolites, these substances aren't technically essential to plant survival, but they play an important indirect role in overall health and fitness, attracting pollinators and seed dispersers, fighting pathogens, and repelling herbivores. When their defenses are breached by caterpillars, beetles, snails, and any number of other creatures, plants recruit parasitoid wasps, birds, and other allies to eat the uninvited guests. Plants can also be good neighbors, releasing volatiles that advertise the presence of nibblers, or they can play poorly with others, emitting toxins that inhibit the growth of nearby species.

In communicating the presence of interlopers, plants don't just sound a general alarm about being munched on, wrote ecologist Keaton Wilson and his coauthors in a 2015 *Bioscience* review paper, "Noisy Communication via Airborne Infochemicals." Their signals can contain information "about presence of below-ground herbivores, about the type of herbivore present on the plant, about pathogen infection, about the development stage of the herbivore, about the number of herbivores present, and about whether or not herbivores have been parasitized."

Though the details of those messages are often cryptic to us, the cries for help can be hard to miss. While hiking in the foothills of Boulder, Colorado, one summer, Ken Keefover-Ring, a biologist and chemical ecologist at the University of Wisconsin, was inundated with odiferous alarm calls, even if he couldn't decipher all their meanings yet. "It was like, wow, I really smell bee balm!" he recalls. "And then I walked down this hill and this population was being eaten like crazy."

Wild bergamot can have a range of scents, recalling oregano, thyme, geranium, eucalyptus, or a sweet floral odor.

Though most herbivores avoid the plant, one-spotted tortoise beetles spend their whole lives on its leaves.

The voracious appetites of one-spotted tortoise beetles had helped him find exactly what he was looking for: stands of *Monarda fistulosa*, a species of bee balm often referred to as wild bergamot and known in Lakota as "sweet-smelling leaf" or "elk medicine." Unlike the insects, though, Keefover-Ring wasn't planning to eat the plant; he just wanted a few leaves for chemical analysis as part of his ongoing graduate school project.

The odor had reached his nose in such abundance because tortoise beetle larvae were grazing on the plants—an effect that Keefover-Ring's experiments later confirmed when he found that chewed-on wild bergamot leaves released twelve times more volatile compounds than those left intact. As members of the mint family, wild bergamot and other bee balms produce strong monoterpenes, the compounds that give essential oils their aroma and flavor, in tiny sacs on their leaves and flowers called trichomes. Just rubbing a leaf is enough to create a powerful scent that keeps most other herbivorous insects and mammals at bay.

Upon closer inspection, Keefover-Ring realized that the tortoise beetle larvae were not only eating the plants but also taking advantage of their defenses to make armor of their own. "I never knew anything about it, and I started looking at these cool little larvae with—as one of my professors called it— a club of crap on their little fork." Constructing a "fecal shield" from his own frass, a larva attaches the turdy tactical gear to a pronged structure at the end of his abdomen and waves it around to scare off anyone with ill intentions.

"How did that evolve? It kind of blows your mind," Keefover-Ring says. "It's really fascinating that they're not only specialists which have evolved to eat bee balm, but then they go one step further; they defend

Larvae of one-spotted tortoise beetles use their terpene-laden frass to construct fecal shields that deter predators.

themselves with it." Many insects are specialists at the larval stage before branching out to a more diverse diet as adults. But one-spotted tortoise beetles spend their whole lives on wild bergamot. Their fecal shields are so chemically concentrated that even years later, Keefover-Ring can still apply a wet finger to his lab books and smell the terpenes.

In his subsequent research, Keefover-Ring found that not all wild bergamot is the same from the tortoise beetle's point of view. Even within the same species, plants can have different chemotypes, meaning that their chemical composition varies from population to population and sometimes even from plant to plant. One common chemotype of wild bergamot is dominated by the terpene thymol,

34

a thyme-scented compound; the other is dominated by carvacrol, which gives oregano its scent. For the animals who rely on these plants, the difference is more than just a slight change in odor. In Keefover-Ring's experiments, tortoise beetles munched on thymol chemotypes more readily, and those who dined on carvacrol chemotypes had lower growth rates and lower survival.

Such outcomes can have far-reaching evolutionary and ecological implications for plants and insects in the wild. Lower herbivory on the more well-defended carvacrol-dominated plants could increase those plants' ability to spread, while a strong preference for the thymol chemotypes might further reduce the tortoise beetles' already extremely limited diet from just one species—wild bergamot—to only a single chemotype of that species.

The findings raise interesting questions about the relationships among plants and animals in our own communities: If a wild bergamot in my garden attracts more insect or deer herbivory than one in my neighbor's, is it because we have different chemotypes? Does a difference in chemotype change which bees visit the flowers? If a native plant of one chemotype is introduced to a natural area where another one dominates, what are the effects on the local plants and fauna? If a gardener plants native seed purchased from a faraway source and is unsure of its origins, as I did a couple of decades ago, does she risk changing the very air that other organisms are used to breathing around that species?

Keefover-Ring has spent his academic career following the scent trails of plants to find answers to these and broader questions about plant ecology and evolutionary history. His interest in wild bergamot was first sparked during another hike in Boulder, when he spotted one of the purple-flowered beauties for the first time, noticed that it had the telltale square stem of plants in the mint family, and inhaled. He'd been working with his adviser on studies of thyme in southern France and recognized the scent. "So I just took a leaf, stuck it in my wallet, and took it back to the lab and soaked it in some solvent," he says. He was so excited that he ran it through an analysis that day. "And sure enough it was thymol; it was the same as a thyme plant."

Gas chromatography and mass spectrometry help scientists separate and identify individual components of scents, but the most relatable way for any of us to describe their essence is to liken them to things we've smelled before. Through chemists, I've come to understand that when my favorite herb, cilantro, goes stale, it smells like the secretions of a common insect because both contain an aldehyde compound known as decenal. But it's my nose that motivates me to keep cilantro fresh in a covered cup of water in the refrigerator, lest my next bite of salsa taste like a mouthful of stinkbugs. Even among seemingly disparate odor sources, our main basis for comparison relies on recall: dog paws and Fritos appear to share the same scent, a quality that McGee notes is likely due to a volatile called aminoacetophenone, which gives corn chips their aroma and also signals the presence of bacteria found in canines and people.

Sniffing out connections and divergences among different populations of wild bergamot and even among individual plants, Keefover-Ring has experienced the thrill of discovery-by-association more than once. In southern Colorado, he found a linalool chemotype, a sweet-smelling compound found in many flowers but unknown in wild bergamot until then. In southern Manitoba, he located a previously identified but rare chemotype dominated by geraniol, the primary monoterpene in the essential oil of some geraniums; the plant was growing among more common thymol and carvacrol chemotypes. More recently in Wisconsin, he found a eucalyptol chemotype at a state park.

The scents weren't new to him; the many olfactory iterations of wild bergamot are also found in the thyme plants he had studied an ocean away. Recent genetic sequencing has closely linked bee balms, thyme, and oregano in a phylogenetic tree of the mint family despite their geographic separation. Keefover-Ring's nose has long told him the plants must have close ties, but the confirmation of his early suspicions sparks new questions: How do the two species relate to each other? Did they diverge from a common ancestor when the continents were still joined, or—maybe more likely—are they the result of convergent evolution, which occurs when unrelated species evolve similar traits that suit their habitats and lifestyles?

A plant's chemical composition can help determine its adaptability and fitness in a given environment. Shared chemotypes of thyme and wild bergamot show resilience in the face of different challenges: the dominance of geraniol has been associated with more resistance to powdery mildew, a common affliction of bee balms. Linalool chemotypes are highly resistant to grasshoppers but less so to other insects. Thyme plants dominated by carvacrol and thymol are good at fending off herbivory and claiming more space for themselves, but they're also more sensitive to cold temperatures.

Though the one-spotted tortoise beetle's single-minded devotion to wild bergamot leaves is not shared by most other plant eaters, the lavender-colored, firecracker-shaped flowers offer a spectacular buffet for hummingbirds, hummingbird moths, fritillaries, swallowtails,

Threatened American bumblebees make a home in our habitat, where they can forage on wildflowers such as ironweed and locate nesting sites among tall dried grasses leftover from previous seasons.

skippers, and bumblebees. Whether the diversity of diners shifts based on the chemical composition of the plant remains to be seen. But at least from the bees' perspective, the flowers offer more than just food. Keefover-Ring's collaborators in Massachusetts have shown that thymol in nectar inhibits internal parasites in bees, "so the bees are kind of medicating themselves," he says. If they're actively using wild bergamot's compounds to stay healthy, bees wouldn't be the only ones, as Indigenous peoples have long used the plant to treat wounds, colds, respiratory problems, and other ailments.

Watching an American bumblebee make a beeline for the wild bergamot and New York ironweeds in our roadside garden, I'm impressed by her concentration. She stays true to her mission, ignoring the passing cars, the camera-toting paparazza, and the acres of blank turf across the street. To locate her lunch, the bee may have had to fly only a few yards from the nearby tufts of tall grasses, one of her preferred nesting sites and an increasingly rare habitat in this land of closely cut lawns. Known scientifically as *Bombus pensylvanicus*, this species has begun vanishing from much of its range over the past two decades and is under consideration for endangered species listing by the US Fish and Wildlife Service. Given their relative rarity in the suburbs and the obstacles they must navigate, the bees' appearance in our habitat is a mystery to me. Even though some of our wildflowers advertise their aromas, how do insects find them amid exhaust fumes, flowerless lawns that disrupt their habitat, and the monoculture farms behind us that scrape and spray away plants all the way to the highway?

Signal Jamming: The Effects of Odor Pollution

Two years before American bumblebees were placed under consideration for federal endangered species protection, I began seeing them in our meadow. Large and fuzzy, they're impossible to miss as they buzz around the deep purple ironweeds and pink field thistles. The first time I spotted one was a sunny August afternoon in 2019, when the singsong voices of children and the laughter of their parents drifted through the trees from next door.

Both the sweet fragrance and ample size
of common milkweed blooms are hard to miss.
Research suggests that bumblebees follow
scent trails to find flower patches and then use
visual cues to glean more information.

Old nests of mice and other rodents are
preferred spots for bumblebee colonies.
Queens likely find them by following
the scents of mouse urine and the natural
materials used in nest construction.

While our human neighbors hosted a barbecue around the fire pit, the wilder neighbors were enjoying their own afternoon snack around our flower patch. But these two sets of partygoers used very different sensory mechanisms to get to their food. For the friends of the family next door, sights and sounds—in the form of a phoned or texted invitation, followed by a drive or walk down familiar roads—had landed them within feet of the appetizing smells emanating from their plates. Scent may have made their mouths water, but it didn't lure them to the party in the first place.

Bumblebees experience a somewhat opposite scenario, with odor playing a critical role in drawing them to the buffet. In a computational modeling study, Jordanna Sprayberry, a professor of biology and neuroscience at Muhlenberg College, found that when foraging for new flowers, bees would have odor information in 90 percent of successful foraging searches, while only 49 percent of successful searches would include visual cues. Upon arrival at a new patch, bees pick up on visual hints, such as colorful patterns that guide them to nectar and changes in bloom color that indicate food availability. But Sprayberry's research suggests that getting close enough to see such cues could require a scent trail, with bumblebees generally spotting visual patterns—especially larger flowers and high densities of plants—only when they're ready to come in for a landing.

Through sensory neurons on their antennae, insects take in odors that their genes have encoded receptors to detect. They follow plant smells to locate food, whether that food is the plant itself or other insects gathering on the plant. Through scent, they can also find mates who congregate on certain plants and locate compounds that enhance their health and defenses. Bumblebees probably even scope out one of their favorite places to nest—abandoned rodent burrows—by following the scent trails of mouse urine and natural materials collected by mice to insulate their young.

Navigating toward an odor's source can be a tricky endeavor, like traveling through an invisible airborne maze. What we see as aimless zigzagging is often a more studied, intentional path that employs multiple senses. Generally flying against the wind to follow an "odor plume"—a mixture of chemicals that forms a recognizable scent—insects use their antennae to determine direction and may also employ a kind of visual steering system to right their paths when veering off course.

Though exquisitely equipped to let their antennal noses lead the way, bees encounter detours and obstacles that can easily obscure their destinations. "All the things that disrupt habitat are going to disrupt air plumes in a lot of ways," says Sprayberry, "because you're no longer looking at an open structure." Environmental pollutants like ozone are another problem, pulling floral odors out of the air and dramatically shortening the distances the plumes can travel. According to one study, a scent that could have been detectable to pollinators from a kilometer or more away during preindustrial times might travel less than two hundred meters today. Air pollution can complicate the picture in other ways, going beyond disrupting odor plumes to causing physiological stress on individual plants, potentially altering the scents they put out into the world.

On top of general air pollution, locally introduced odors can further obscure natural floral signals. A 2013 UK study found that when floral chemicals were exposed to diesel exhaust, the scents were so altered that few honeybees could recognize them anymore. The same year, Sprayberry published research showing the negative effects of the scent of agrochemicals, the first study of its kind. In lab experiments, the presence of a fungicide confused bumblebees, increasing the time they took to navigate toward floral odors. When given the choice, they also showed a significant preference for fresh-air pathways over those contaminated by common lawn fertilizer.

Armed with those results, Sprayberry set out to quantify the pollution potential of other lawn and garden chemicals, a trip down a "rabbit hole" that took seven years. The study of scent interactions may be the most ambitious undertaking in all of sensory ecology. Unlike color and tone—which are measured in wavelength and intensity, frequency and volume—odor is more reactive and directionless, lacking universal baselines and subject to the whims of the winds. Scent molecules are hydrophobic, helping odor plumes stick together, but air turbulence can disperse them across the landscape. Add to that an extraordinary number of scent receptors—400 for humans and 170 for honeybees, for example, compared with each species' three color receptors—and the possible interactions among senders and receivers seem limitless.

"When we look at odor, what is the difference between a molecule in bleach or sulfuric acid and one of the thirty-plus molecules that come off a cup of coffee?" asks Sprayberry. Many signals combine to form our perception and identification of a given scent, and there's no straightforward way to quantify them yet. "Roses can have up to two hundred scent molecules, and what is the relationship? There's no relationship."

In her quest to identify possible disruptors of natural scents in the landscape, Sprayberry found herself staring down a list of more than eight hundred lawn and garden products at a single big-box store. Testing the impacts of each one, she realized, would be a never-ending task. So she flipped the problem around to look at it from the perspective of insect olfactory systems, developing a model for predicting the points at which their scent receptors can no longer distinguish between a food resource and a pollutant. "Now that we have that, we can start to ask more questions like, 'What is the difference between a scent and its background? At what level does a scent become part of the background? When is pollution perceived as a separate odor or a joined odor?'"

To explain the concept to her students, Sprayberry resorts to a cooking metaphor: come to her house for dinner, and the first thing you might smell is onions slowly cooking in olive oil. Carrots, garlic, and celery may enhance the scent, but probably not beyond recognition. "Then I add sage, and then I add tomatoes, and then I add lentils. That no longer smells like the same thing," she says. "But at what point did it shift its identity? That's really mushy, versus if you come over, and there's a cup of bleach open on the counter, and you're like, 'Why are you ruining the smell of dinner with bleach?'"

An ability to recognize shared traits amid the "mushiness" is actually helpful to pollinators, says Sprayberry, enabling them to follow sufficiently familiar odor plumes that are most likely to get them to the flowers they need. "There's a level of pollution where it's OK that it's polluted—that we have these other odors, but I'm still treating it with the same intent. But there's a level of pollution where you push it too far, and the animals no longer treat it like the signal they learned." In a second study on the effects of fungicides, Sprayberry and her colleagues found that the chemicals' odors decreased bumblebees' ability to learn and recognize the floral scent of wild bergamot.

Wild bergamot is an insect hot spot even at night, when the flowers shelter sleeping carpenter bees and bumblebees. Research shows that fungicides can disrupt bees' ability to learn and recognize the scent of the blooms.

Insects are finely tuned for efficient foraging; at close range, bumblebees can even detect the footprints of previous flower visitors, a social odor cue alerting them that the keg has already been tapped. To find those flowers in the first place, a powerful fragrance is key but not always as discernible across large landscapes. Even food crops and nonnative plants might be significant disruptors, emitting odors that could confuse insects or mask the scents of local species.

Habitat loss and fragmentation exacerbate pollution problems. "We are actively increasing distances between habitat patches," says

The strong scents emitted by dense plantings of species like mountain mint—shown here with a leafcutter bee and a metallic-green sweat bee—might cut through the noise of odor pollution.

When odor pollution has diminished bees' abilities to sniff out flowers, large blooms—like those of purple coneflower—can serve as beacons.

Sprayberry. "And if you add these two together in a suburban or urban environment, you've taken food resources, you've spread them out, and you've added air pollution that drops the distance at which these signals can travel. Then you're really reducing the amount of resources animals can gather in a foraging trip."

Sprayberry's computational study showed that when potential contact with floral odor plumes decreased, bumblebees were more successful at locating those patches that were packed with plants. They "may passively select for larger bloom size and higher plant density in polluted environments," she wrote, "by virtue of not being able to locate smaller flowers" or flowers that are farther away. Encouraging thick spreading of scented native species, including those with smaller blooms such as mountain mints, might help bees find their dinner. An assist from visual cues—in the form of large patches packed with big blooms and tall plants—could also serve as a beacon, a floral lighthouse beaming on the edges of the unknown.

Monarch Mysteries: Decoding a Secret Language

Boneset is a plant that stands out from the crowd, sometimes reaching great heights to find the light. When it appeared one year in our front patch near the road, I watched with increasing fascination as it grew and grew all summer, Jack-and-the-Beanstalk style, before finally flowering just in time to welcome migrating monarchs on their autumn journey to Mexico.

Since then, the progeny of that one pioneering plant, known scientifically as *Eupatorium serotinum*, have made themselves at home across our habitat. In some years, the boneset blooms smell sweeter than roses; in others, they're milder. Plant scent signals are dynamic even among individuals, depending on soil conditions, temperature, age, and time of year. Flowers can change their scent profiles from morning to night.

Throughout our gardens, the bonesets have become gathering places for ailanthus moths, pearl crescents, Eastern-tailed blues, and common buckeye butterflies, whose beautiful blue-and-orange eye-spots remind me of impressionist cityscapes at sunset. The eye-level white blooms have offered an up-close look at gorgeous blue-winged wasps, thread-waisted wasps, and sand-loving wasps—all self-appointed guardians who protect plants by picking off would-be leaf nibblers like caterpillars, grasshoppers, and beetle larvae and carrying them to their own nests, where baby wasps will eventually feed on the hapless insects. Thanks to the prolific boneset, we've gotten to know the fuzzy, so-ugly-they're-cute large tachinid flies with spiky exteriors and their daintier tachinid cousins, the feather-legged flies, who sport fake pollen baskets to disguise themselves. These parasitoids, who lay their eggs on or near other insects, are considered bee mimics, but to me they don't look quite like bees or flies, just strangely beautiful creatures in their own right.

Given all the life swirling around the beckoning blooms, it never occurred to me that the bonesets would still have something to offer to insects even after they decay and die, or that their leaves might be as attractive as flowers to a butterfly. But one recent summer, the plants and animals who have long been my teachers had a new lesson plan in store for me.

On a warm June evening, an aimless wander through the front garden led me toward a male monarch sitting on a boneset leaf.

Tachinid flies (above) and pearl crescents are among the many interesting creatures drawn to boneset blooms.

Assuming he was resting, I lazily lifted my camera and soon realized that this was no perching butterfly. The monarch was hard at work, sinking his proboscis into the leaf and rubbing it with one of his feet as if trying to coax out more of whatever goodness lay inside. The occasional passing car startled him into the air and over the common milkweeds in full bloom. But he ignored his favorite flowers and quickly returned to the task at hand.

My curiosity piqued, I posted a video clip and questions to an insect group on social media: Why was a butterfly probing a leaf instead of a nectar-filled bloom? What could he possibly hope to gain from that? And if he was extracting something valuable, how did he even find it? Why did he choose this particular leaf? A reply came quickly from retired Smithsonian lepidopterist Don Harvey, who sent me a link to a 1983 paper, "Leaf-Scratching: A Specialized Behaviour of Danaine Butterflies (Lepidoptera) for Gathering Secondary Plant Substances."

Almost four decades before, the author, a German chemical ecologist named Michael Boppré, had described watching the same behavior in Kenya among related species in the Danaini tribe, known as the milkweed butterflies. He'd even noticed that the winged beauties had received some help from much tinier and less-loved creatures in locating the plants: "Almost all leaves of the *Heliotropium* population had holes of varying diameter (1-4 mm) made by flea beetles," he wrote. "Close inspection of leaves which were only slightly damaged by butterflies revealed that the danaines had scratched radially from these holes, and it appears that the edges of the holes release the chemical cues responsible for attraction of danaines." How exciting it was to reexamine my videos and find that many thousands of miles away

Monarchs, like others in the Danaini tribe, extract pyrrolizidine alkaloids (PAs) from injured, decaying, and dead plants to fortify their own defenses. When PA-containing plants' cell walls break down and atmospheric conditions are right, a scent is released that attracts the butterflies.

and years later, these much-maligned beetles appeared to be helping butterflies in our habitat too: along the top of the leaf that the monarch was busily probing, a flea beetle ambled about before disappearing to the underside!

Throughout his career, Boppré had studied the phenomenon among many insects, particularly tiger and wasp moths in Latin America. From his papers I learned the term *pharmacophagy*, which refers to the gathering of substances from plant parts for reasons unrelated to nutrition. Some plant species produce pyrrolizidine alkaloids (PAs) to protect themselves from herbivory, an effective strategy in our habitat, where the bonesets generally go untouched by deer and rabbits. But insects of many kinds—including not just certain butterflies and moths but also some grasshopper, beetle, and fly species—have found a way to co-opt PAs to their advantage, synthesizing them into pheromones for courtship and sequestering them for defense against predators and parasitoids. Describing the monarchs' motivations from a human perspective, Boppré used this analogy: the butterflies treat wildflowers and larval host plants as their "grocery stores," and they use PA-containing plants as their "drugstores."

The more I read, the more perplexing my observation seemed, and if I hadn't seen it with my own eyes, I might not have believed it. Though PA-gathering is common among their closest relatives, American monarchs are rarely mentioned in scientific discussions of the behavior, and usually only as an exception to the rule. A passage in one recent book described PA sequestration among virtually all other studied butterfly species in the milkweed butterfly tribe but neglected to mention PA-gathering as an important facet of monarchs' life history. Authors of a 2020 study declared that butterflies in the *Danaus* genus, including monarchs, "do not perform leaf-scratching" in the Americas and that monarchs "are not attracted to vegetative PA sources."

If that were really the case, the reasons seem sensible enough on their face, given the most commonly relayed life history of the species: as caterpillars, monarchs eat milkweed exclusively. While digesting the green leafy bits, they also sequester cardiac glycosides, substances that provide lifelong defense against antagonists. Because of this special

Reports of other butterfly species gathering PAs have involved mostly males, but I've seen female monarchs doing so at least twice. Here a male and female are busy on a half-broken boneset.

talent for commandeering toxins from milkweed for long-term protection, many monarchs are already well defended. And unlike males of related species who synthesize PAs into courtship pheromones, male monarchs don't seem to employ such romantic preambles. In adulthood, they imbibe only from flowers, not withering leaves. End of story, or so we had been led to believe.

By the next summer, I realized my monarchs might be rewriting the American scientific narrative about their species when I again

Monarchs can extract PAs not just from leaves but also from stems and dried flowers.

Unlike related butterfly species that modify PAs into courtship pheromones, monarchs don't appear to use them for that purpose.

encountered them probing leaves. Their chosen plants were dry, brown, and shriveled, and I'd been meaning to cut them down due to arbitrary human concerns: worries about how a dead plant in the front garden would look to my neighbors and regrets that a half-broken one in the back marred my lush garden photos.

The monarchs had no such concerns as they went about extracting PAs from dead and withering leaves and stems. A lone female by the roadside was so goal-oriented that she continued for at least forty-five minutes. A week later, a male and female gathered PAs for ten minutes in the meadow, flying about to nectar on goldenrod and mountain mint when they were done. Excited about the repeat sightings, I contacted a well-known scientist to find out why no one else was reporting this and what it could mean. The reply was a dead end, as the researcher brushed off my observations as likely a vestigial behavior, one that may have meant something to the monarchs' ancestors but had no relevance to the species now.

How could that be, I wondered, given how much time the monarchs were spending on the leaves? In the coming seasons I would see monarchs on dried plants for up to an hour at a time. Insects don't have energy to waste; why would they invest it in something they don't need? Finding the ephemeral scent of the senescing plants in the first place can be a drawn-out endeavor, taking hours or days or weeks. And if a plant is dry, a butterfly can't access the PAs until he first moistens the leaves by regurgitating his own fluid; even then, he won't be able to re-imbibe all the liquid. "It's a costly behavior," Boppré told me when I eventually reached out to him for help in unraveling my monarch mystery. "They wouldn't do it if it didn't make sense to them."

PA pharmacophagy among monarchs is context-specific and not a universal trait, but the conditions under which individuals engage in it are still unknown. How the butterflies zero in on their drug supply is also unclear, says Boppré, but "it can be nothing else than an odor." The scent released when PA-containing plants break down can be so attractive and powerful that it seems to draw insects out of the blue. When Boppré once pulled up to a small forest near a river, prepared with lures made of dried leaves, no butterflies were on the wing. "I take a bait out of the car," he recalled, "and Danaini appear within minutes." Bob Robbins, curator of lepidoptera at the Smithsonian Institution, witnessed the irresistibility of PAs in Peru when 150 males of 20 to 30 tropical clearwing butterfly species gathered on cut PA-containing plants hung from trees. On another outing in the Amazon, a friend opened a container of purified extracts of PA-containing plants, and "all of a sudden the males of these ctenuchid moths—which are a group of tiger moths—would start dive-bombing us," Robbins said. "It was remarkable!"

But the volatiles detected by chemoreceptors in insect antennae appear to have no discernible scent to human noses and have been too ephemeral for chemists to capture and analyze. In intact leaves, PAs are concealed. Only when the cell walls start to break down, either through senescence or nibbling by insects, do the compounds separate and react with the ambient atmosphere, producing an inviting but elusive scent through hydrolysis. Some evidence exists that the attractant may be necine alcohol based, but no one really knows, says Boppré. "Because it's such a short-lived molecule and so reactive, for twenty or thirty years we've tried to find it, and we cannot catch it."

A female monarch lays tiny pearl-like eggs. It's possible that monarchs pass along PAs in their eggshells, as the related queen butterflies are known to do, conferring short-term protection against parasites to larvae who may consume the shells after hatching.

It's not clear how PAs help the monarchs beyond generally fortifying their defenses, but Boppré has a theory: perhaps they protect offspring from infection by a devastating protozoan parasite that's been spreading more intensively among monarch populations in recent years. Called *Ophryocystis elektroscirrha* (OE), it can weaken butterflies, stunt and crumple their wings, and ultimately lead to shortened lives. The spores drop off the bodies of adult butterflies onto milkweed, where caterpillars ingest them and become infected. But if a monarch mother has taken up PAs, the compounds may be present in the shells of the eggs she has lain; early-stage caterpillars, who are sometimes known to eat those shells, may gain sufficient protection to fend off OE sporozoites. "We have no idea," says Boppré, "but that might be a very plausible reason why monarchs take up PAs, and maybe only when they are heavily infected."

By the time I spoke with Boppré, he'd been puzzling over some of the same questions about the dearth of data: Why weren't there more reports of this important behavior? Why did Americans seem to ignore the ecology of PA-gathering even though scientists had identified the compounds in the bodies of monarchs in California and Mexico? Previous sightings of monarchs gathering PAs in the United States were sparse, confined to two observations: one in Florida in 1975, when a scientist watched them probing dried leaves in a baited butterfly trap, and one in Missouri in 2009, when a gardener photographed monarchs probing the roots of an upturned exotic pond species. But other than those reports and mine, Boppré said, "We have no natural history observations from the United States."

Pharmacophagy is likely common among monarchs in North America; my garden can't be the only place it's occurring repeatedly and for long durations. It'll take many more observations, combined with controlled experiments, to solve the mystery of monarchs and their relationship with PAs. We decided to accelerate the process by writing a paper for the scientific community and launching a community science project, Monarch Rx. Plants in the United States known to contain pyrrolizidine alkaloids occur in at least nine genera—*Artemisia, Amsinckia, Chromolaena, Crotalaria, Erechtites, Eupatorium, Hackelia, Heliotropium,* and *Senecio*—and continued sightings of monarchs visiting these species can help us learn about more. Data from keen observers can also help determine whether males and females are attracted to PAs in equal measure, how often and how long they visit the plants, and which weather conditions and habitat elements might fill the air with that elusive and irresistible scent that's beyond our own ability to detect.

Coming Full Circle

When we received notice that our paper would be published, it had been five days since my father had died of a massive stroke. "It is a pleasure to accept your manuscript entitled 'The puzzle of monarch butterflies (*Danaus plexippus*) and their association with plants containing pyrrolizidine alkaloids' in its current form for publication in *Ecological Entomology*," the email read. "We look forward to your continued contributions."

My mind drifted to a time decades ago when my dad saw me observing ants in the garden and teased, "I'm going to make a scientist out of you yet!" A plant virologist, he encouraged my teenage ambitions to be a writer but would have been just as happy if I'd joined him in the lab and greenhouses. Though he didn't live to see my byline in a scientific journal, I'd had a chance to tell him about my latest discovery one fall day a few months before he died, as we worked in his garden. He could no longer bend down safely to plant his beloved tulips, so he dug holes with a long shovel while I tucked the bulbs into the earth. He was as nurturing and curious and loving and particular as always, asking questions to prompt me to keep talking. "I think that's amazing, Nancy! How did you figure this out? Why hadn't anyone seen it before? Oh, you can move that bulb just a little to the right! That's it! Thank you, dear!"

In his own way, my father did train me to become a scientist, passing along a curiosity, patience, and attention to detail I've only recently come to appreciate as qualities worth cultivating. There are no letters after my name, but there are also no constraints in my brain from existing bodies of research, no peer pressure from the halls of academia to tell me how the world should and shouldn't be. Without the internalized skeptic's voice that can come with years of increasing specialization in a given field, you are more free to be like a bumblebee—or a monarch butterfly—and just follow your eyes and your nose and, if you're lucky enough to catch it, the scent on the winds. As Diane Ackerman notes in *A Natural History of the Senses*: "Mastery is what we strive for, but once we have it we lose the precarious super-awareness of the amateur."

Monarchs spend much of their lives aloft. Unlike many other butterflies, they don't overwinter as caterpillars, eggs, or chrysalises under leaves or in grasses; in fact, except in California and the Deep South, they don't overwinter in the United States at all but instead fly to

Mexico to huddle up in the trees. For most of us, opportunities to observe them are restricted to a few weeks a year.

Yet they're so familiar, and so enmeshed in the popular culture and in conservation programs, that we might be tempted to think there isn't anything more to learn about them. As I navigated through the research, I was struck by how much we don't know about even iconic animals—monarchs are among the most studied butterflies in the world—and how easy it is for people who keep their eyes and mind open to push against the edges of scientific knowledge about our wild neighbors.

A few days after I published a post on my website about the debut of Monarch Rx, I heard from Brice. We'd been pen pals for more than a year, sending each other letters, emails, books, and photos of our latest sightings. Now thirteen, Brice had fully immersed himself in nature advocacy over the past year, producing a video on monarchs with his little sister, Coco; creating a website with eloquent posts about the lifestyles of native bees, the importance of native plants, and the devastating effects of fishing line and red tide on wildlife; earning the distinction of having the most bee observations on iNaturalist in the state of Florida; and finding a little-known wasp species five feet from his front door. His photos and observations are so good that scientists and graduate students now call him for help in their research. And in his latest email, he was already contributing to mine too:

Hi Nancy,

I was reading your newest article today and was so excited to realize I have seen monarchs collecting pyrrolizidine alkaloids in our

The young naturalist Brice Claypoole was the first to submit a sighting of a monarch gathering PAs on dried joe-pye weed to our citizen science project, Monarch Rx.

After he began leaving out dead stalks of plants, Brice noticed that Eastern Slosson's cuckoo leafcutter bees used the decaying material for roosting at night in his garden.

yard!! I thought there must have been nectar still left in the long dead blooms of the joe-pye weed (which is apparently closely related to boneset), but now I know! We sent this to some friends who might be interested. I've included pictures of the monarch collecting PAs.

Brice

Brice had the distinction of being the first person to upload a valid observation onto Monarch Rx. He'd watched the monarch the year before and couldn't understand why a butterfly would want to visit a dried-up wildflower. "He had just read your book in the spring," his mom, Ali Claypoole, told me, "and was really pushing to create more habitat and plant natives and to leave things."

Brice chimed in as the three of us caught up on Zoom one day. "Before I read your book, I would have totally taken that joe-pye down months before the monarch got to it!" After he'd started to leave seedheads for birds and dead stalks for cavity-nesting bees, Brice made yet another discovery of his own: that male long-horned bees were roosting together on dried plants—and only the dried ones—every night. Later he observed Eastern Slosson's cuckoo leafcutter bees lining up on the same stalk to sleep when evening fell, something he found sweet until he looked a little closer and saw one of nature's many competitive scrambles. "They'll stomp on each other, and they're like, 'That's my spot, that's my spot,'" he said, "and the biggest one always gets the favored spot."

Though I've been leaving fallen logs and leaves and leftover stalks for years in my wildlife habitat, I was just as surprised as Brice to learn of even more ways that butterflies and bees could use such detritus too. Nature has shown us both that there's more life after death than we could have imagined—including on decaying and broken wildflowers still standing and still sending their invisible scents into the aerosphere, a final gift to the animals during their descent back into the earth.

CHAPTER 2

The Soundscape

Silence is not the absence of something
but the presence of everything.
—Gordon Hempton

The green frog speaks authoritatively, belting out self-assured clucks followed by descending staccato notes, aural ellipses that leave me hanging on every word. He's not as loud as his higher-pitched relatives, the tiny gray tree frogs serenading from the canopy, but his deep voice travels farther, penetrating the walls of our house. Sometimes he's protecting his territory; other times he's calling for a mate. I like to pretend he's calling for me as I head down to the pond.

Many voices compete for our attention during these seasons of political and cultural reckoning, and some days they split my mind into more lines of thought than I can follow, flashflooding an already saturated brain space. It's in those moments that I seek the company and clarity of someone untethered to human society and unaware of the latest farces and failures of compassion and common sense that assault us in the daily news—a creature with a natural affinity for knowing when to speak up and when to bask in the silence.

We hadn't even finished laying the stones when green frogs began calling our new pond home.

The green frogs' deep voices reverberate throughout the landscape, aided by vocal sacs that amplify the sound.

In June, we carved the green frog's watery home out of an old turf patch next to regenerating woodland, and he found it before we'd even finished stacking the last stones. The next spring came a succession of different species: peeping spring peepers and clucking wood frogs mating in March, trilling American toads hopping out of the leaves in April, tree frog sopranos climbing into the canopy in May, and green frogs chattering away again all summer long.

Just as there's a natural order to the frogs' successive emergence, there's also a pattern to when they sing their songs. Known to biologists and nature recordists as "acoustic partitioning," the sharing of the soundscape among animals plays out like a finely composed symphony. In nature's orchestra, according to the theories of soundscape pioneer Bernie Krause, animals occupy different niches, vocalizing at alternating times and frequencies so all can be heard.

Each spot on Earth has its own acoustic patterns, unique to the organisms and geographic features present, even in a suburban patch like mine. Nowhere else do silver maple branches sway in autumn morning winds to brush the shoulders of the Eastern red cedar, in whose arms the cardinals, sparrows, and juncos hide between turns at the birdbath. Nowhere else does the summer rain keep falling in the sassafras grove by the driveway long after the sun reappears, the trees shaking themselves off to the tune of the little girl singing through the woods from the house next door. There may be coyotes yipping, foxes screaming, owls hooting, and squirrels chittering down the street, but they aren't mixing the way they do here with the chirping crickets and operatic wrens and cooing mourning doves.

Listening to natural soundscapes "rivets us to the present tense— to life as it is—singing in its full-throated choral voice and where each singer is expressing its particular song of being," Krause wrote in his book *Voices of the Wild*. Commanding my attention even when I've forgotten to look, the sound of the green frog's voice throughout the landscape reminds me that I'm never alone. Unlike sight, sound surrounds us, needing no invitation, as acoustician and naturalist Michael Stocker reminded us in *Hear Where We Are*: "Sight works in straight lines—we need to direct our vision to something in order to perceive it. On the other hand, hearing is hemispherical; we hear sounds from all around, not just where we cast our ears."

For those of us with fewer than two functioning ears, hearing may better be described as semihemispherical. I am mostly deaf on the right side, and my hearing loss limits detection of the full frequency range; it's difficult to glean high notes, where the consonants tend to lie. Stereo sound is nonexistent, sometimes to comical and dizzying effect when I spin around hopelessly to pinpoint who's calling my name. Spatial awareness, balance, and diction are all more challenging, as is the ability to judge volume: all my life, everyone from my grandmothers to my husband has said I'm speaking either too softly or too loudly—a mumbler or a shouter, depending on background noise, with few in-betweens. Perhaps most challenging of all is the inability to hear punch lines in a group setting amid background noise; even if the joke's on me, I wouldn't know it.

None of this has muted my joy or gratefulness for the sounds that remain; many people are half-deaf and appear no worse for wear, and some well-functioning animals are also off-balance. I felt a kinship with the tiny owlet moths in my garden when I learned that in at least one species, individuals zigzag around with mites hanging out in a single ear; the mites climb onto the moths from flowers and stick to only one side, possibly with the help of pheromone trails to keep each other on track. It's a great strategy: if the parasites went after both ears, everyone would go down in an attack, ending up in the gullet of a bat out foraging for his midnight snack. By leaving one side alone, ear mites save themselves by saving the moths, who can still sense the bat sonar with their only good ear and escape being eaten.

Though I too have adapted to my lopsidedness, understanding the effects of hearing loss inspires empathy for the struggles of other creatures communicating against a background of unnatural noise. In biological terms, overcompensating for any sensory deprivation or deficit creates energy costs; the mental exertion required to hear and relay messages can be fatiguing and corrosive of other cognitive functions. Friends and colleagues have long teased me about my "six-second delay" (which over time has expanded to twelve seconds)—a response time we all thought was due to my intense focus and an inability to mentally transition quickly between topics. I now realize there's probably more to it: I'm simply buying time while I piece together context, vowels, and lip movements to figure out what someone is actually saying.

For species more dependent on vocal communication, the consequences of noise disruption are far reaching. The negative effects of our human-made cacophony reverberate across the animal kingdom, affecting everyone from mollusks to mammals, and can lead to reproductive failure, an increased vulnerability to predators, and the inability to find prey or locate mates. In field studies and experimental work, researchers have found that chronic noise can result in reduced egg hatching in bluebirds and tree swallows, decreased foraging efficiency of owls and bats, lower presence of insects and spiders, and

Researchers have found that bluebirds have less nesting success in the presence of anthropogenic noise.

delayed response to frog mating calls. As loud as our frogs are, their natural vocal ranges may be no match for the drone of road traffic and airplanes; studies suggest that amid such background noise, females could take longer to locate mates, who may need to change their call rates or raise their pitches to be heard. Some birds appear to give up entirely and search for greener pastures; research in Idaho showed that sounds of traffic caused a 28 percent drop in bird abundance, and a continent-wide analysis of community science data revealed that many birds avoid noisy areas altogether. By altering the behaviors of pollinators and seed dispersers, noise can even limit plant growth and change the very structure of a forest.

For now, my green frog friend and I can still hear each other, and our conversations are straightforward. Though most of his compatriots are wary of my presence and dip underwater when I round the path, my favorite chatterbox seems to have the opposite reaction, usually speaking up and sometimes even swimming toward me as I plant seedlings near the pond's edge. Occasionally he hops up on a nearby rock and keeps me company as I work, showing off his tympanums, which sit behind his eyes and are twice as large—a size that indicates his male status. These round membranes are eardrums, keeping water and debris out while transmitting sound to his inner ears. Whether we understand each other's words is debatable, but each summer I learn a little bit more about his language, and I have come to realize that his typical greeting might be nothing more and nothing less than a hearty hello: "Good morning! Here I am, and this is my song."

Learning to Listen

The bench on the edge of our pond marks a border between two worlds. In front of me is a forest in the making, where brown thrashers churn the leaves, Carolina wrens snatch moths from midair, and red-shouldered hawks perch in the tulip trees, waiting for their moment. Behind me is a land bereft, a carnage of stumps where, one after the other, nesting sites for bluebirds and owls have met their doom in the yards of neighbors who expand their own houses but

Brown thrashers hide and nest among dense vegetation and can be difficult to spot, but you might hear them sweeping their bills through leaves as they forage for insects.

The echoing drums of the pileated woodpecker are a welcome exclamation point in the soundscape, indicating high-quality habitat filled with trees and dead wood harboring ants and other treats.

declare war on leafy green homes they've deemed too tall or too disruptive of their acres of turf.

Eventually they'll call in the hitmen to take out the last of the stumps too, leaving little left for the woodpeckers who feast on insects in dead wood and sending everyone else fleeing from the deafening roar of life being ground up. Noise often begets noise, and as trees disappear, so do nature's buffers. The gas-powered chainsaws, the crashing down of their stately victims, the assault on their remains—all these sounds might be considered short-lived, but the screaming machinery we hear when forests die is only the beginning. In the aftermath of destruction here and along the nearby interstates, where miles of trees have given way all summer to new driving lanes, a low-frequency grind signals the internal combustion engines that have free range to trample across the open landscape. When weather conditions are right, traffic from the once-distant highways grows so loud that it sometimes feels like tractor trailers are ripping their way through our backyard. The nights when cool air gives way to warm fronts are the worst, and as I roll over on my good ear to try to block out the intrusion, I've often wondered how animals outside can get any good shut-eye at all. It's a question scientists in Belgium recently tackled, showing that traffic noise has significant negative effects on European songbirds called great tits, reducing how long they sleep and prompting them to leave their nest boxes earlier in the morning.

But on this mild October evening, all is quiet on the tiny western front of our habitat. A rare equilibrium of temperature and winds, combined with recent rains, keeps highway noise away and power tools at bay. Without the backdrop of whining trucks and grating

Stumps left for woodpeckers encourage beautiful fungi and create habitat for native cavity-nesting bees and other insects.

rumble strips and machine-happy neighbors, even the softest sounds can fall on my half-deaf ears and actually be heard.

I've come here to actively listen, as I do nearly every day now in an attempt to understand the many languages and expressions of my wild neighbors. People often describe animals as having no voice, citing this as a reason to advocate for them. Many organizations make it part of their motto, saying they are "the voice of the voiceless" or that they're "speaking up for those who can't speak for themselves." Even though such phrasings are intended as metaphors for animals' inability to participate in human power structures and decision-making, they do a disservice by obscuring a greater truth: far from being mute, the natural world has an incalculable array of voices, including those we can hear and those that are well beyond our range. But we just haven't taken the time to listen—and worse, we're drowning them out before any of us alive today has even begun to comprehend the full chorus.

What do we lose when we can no longer hear nature? Natural sounds have proven positive effects on our health, lowering stress levels and increasing our resilience. One experiment showed that even brief bouts of exposure to quiet birdsong, played from strategic places along a park trail, created a significant subconscious boost to the moods of hikers when compared with hikers walking on a trail with fewer bird voices. "It's amazing," says Clinton Francis, associate professor at Cal Poly State University and the lead author of the study. "In seven minutes you can see a measurable effect on people's indirect, self-reported well-being."

Yet we shut out the world around us—and sometimes permanently shut down our own senses—by turning up the volume and lowering our heads into screens that have caused an epidemic of myopia, in more ways than one. No sense is safe from our neglect: in studies designed to measure the value that young people place on their technology, about half said they would rather lose their sense of smell or break a bone than lose their electronic devices—the chronic use of which can damage their hearing and vision too. Only a century ago, school primers described everyday sounds and sights outside: milkweed seedpods blowing in the wind, robins singing, violets blooming, and goldenrods with buzzing bees lining the lanes where maple leaves crunched underfoot. Now mowers and pesticides have made such rich sensory scenes foreign to many children, a heartbreaking reality reflected in a decision by editors of the *Oxford Junior Dictionary* to erase them from the vernacular, expunging words like *raven* and *willow* to make way for *broadband*, *blog*, and other fashionable terms of the machine-driven world.

Surrounded throughout the seasons by beings who have outlasted all manner of human invention, I honor the ones who've been disappeared from that dictionary by rereading Robert Macfarlane and Jackie Morris's wondrous book *The Lost Words* and going outside to whisper their names out loud: a *heron* who lands on my neighbor's roof, surveying the ponds. A Carolina *wren* who lands in the birdbath for a good soak that ruffles her feathers. The *brambles* where tanagers, blue jays, bluebirds, and red-bellied woodpeckers feed and hide. The *ferns* I transplanted from my father's garden to the pond, where a frog wraps his legs around the fronds and holds on tight. The *acorns* that deer eat in fall and that squirrels and chipmunks stash away for emergencies. The *dandelions* that rabbits and groundhogs happily nibble to nubs.

Far from receding into the shadows of human memory, the animals take center stage whenever I sit in silence long enough. One late summer afternoon, a juvenile rabbit comes into view, hops down the path toward me, leaps onto my flip-flop, and sits under the bench for a while. Another night she stops in front of me, lies down, and stretches out on the wood-chipped path like a dog relaxing on a sofa, back legs kicked out in meditative repose. Chickadees and tufted titmice have landed on my shoulder and pecked around on the bench within inches of me, frogs mate in full view, and turtles lay eggs as if no one is watching.

Rustling leaves are the sounds of industry in nature.

This evening, a squirrel who's been wandering through the flowers ambles straight to the bench and stops short at the sight of my new red boots. Holding a walnut between his front paws and looking slowly up at my face, he seems to consider his options—*Who is this, and will she steal my food?*—before diverting to the path, pretending to dig a hole, and disappearing out of view. I can't see him, but I still hear him, and I detect hints of ingenuity and preplanning: a squirrel burying his winter stash, following in the footsteps of a predecessor who planted the small walnut tree that has shaded me here all summer. Though I dare not turn around to peek, I don't need to; the commotion behind me, imperceptible on noisier days, is unmistakable now.

"Rustling leaves" are so quiet they're often cited as an example of near-silence on the low end of decibel charts, with their destroyers—leaf blowers—at the other extreme end of the scale. In fact, until I learned to sit still for longer than a few minutes, I couldn't conjure very well what the phrase meant. "Crackling leaves" were more familiar, a rhythm from my childhood days when I spent hours playing among curbside piles on my way home from school. We humans crackle leaves with our hands, and we crunch them underfoot. But what does it mean to rustle?

The word has an uncertain origin, possibly from the German *ruschen*, and is defined by the Cambridge Dictionary as "to emit soft, rapid sounds." *Rustle*'s other definition—"to steal"—may be an American-made mashup of "rush" and "hustle." Both meanings are applicable when it comes to squirrels, who are known to bury, dig up, and rebury their nuts; sometimes they even just pretend to stow away supplies as a way to deceive lurking ne'er-do-wells like me.

What else causes leaves to rustle, besides squirrelly industriousness? Even more than the birdsong above, the commotion in the leaves is what first began to ground me to this place and time, cluing me in to what's happening right at my feet. Rustling leaves, I've come to understand, are the sounds of white-throated sparrows kicking up layers to reveal insect and seed treats underneath. Rustling leaves are the warmup notes of toads emerging from a long winter nap, a sometimes sudden and startling affair that leads to mass orgies of frantic males piling atop one another on our patio, under our deck, and in the ponds. They're the winding-down sounds of trees announcing it's time to go to sleep. If you're an owl tuning in for rodents at midnight, rustling leaves are the sweet sound of dinner.

To get to the point of rustling on the ground, though, a leaf must be allowed to fall, turn brown, and wither away on its own time, without being raked or shredded or blown away—the landscaping version of invasive cosmetic surgery. To rustle in the canopy, a tree must be allowed to grow tall, branch out, and be heard by someone, anyone, whether four-footed, six-footed, eight-footed, or two.

Recovering the Lost Words of Birds

Nature recordist Lang Elliott was in college before he realized he couldn't hear the rustling understory. Walking along the limestone bluffs of Devils Backbone, Missouri, he was surprised when his friend repeatedly pointed out fence lizards near the path. "Finally I asked him, 'How are you spotting these things?' He said, 'I'm not spotting these things. I hear them running in the leaves.'"

Other than assuming his friend had exceptional hearing, Elliott didn't think much of it—until graduate school, when he walked along Maryland's Severn River with a professor who specialized in bird sounds and saw a worm-eating warbler. "We ended up under a tree, watching the bird sing its heart out, and it would throw back its head, open up its beak, and let out this sound, and I couldn't hear it at all." He also couldn't hear the high-pitched sounds of the flying squirrels he was studying, and whenever he dropped a coin from his pocket, others had to alert him to it.

Subsequent tests revealed that Elliott couldn't hear anything above a frequency—or pitch—of three thousand hertz, the consequence of a cherry bomb exploding over his head when he was thirteen. People with typical hearing can detect sounds from twenty to twenty thousand hertz. Though Elliott's hearing had been tested after the fireworks accident and he'd been told never to join a rock band, no one had mentioned that he suffered from profound hearing loss, rendering him unable to detect half to two-thirds of birds' songs.

"It was a heartbreaker," recalls Elliott, who eventually became one of the nation's most prominent documentarians of natural sounds. "It crushed me. I was so upset about it, and I couldn't believe I was missing all this stuff."

Already pursuing his dream of being a field biologist, Elliott couldn't imagine studying animals whose voices he couldn't hear. Hearing aids would only amplify the detectable sounds, including background noise, while still excluding those pitches that were out of his range. After learning in bird classes at Cornell University that songs recorded at high speed drop in pitch when played back more slowly, he came up with an idea: Why not design an instrument that would relay birdsongs at lower pitches in real time? Working with engineers, he created a series of devices before landing on one that was so small it could be carried in a pocket but so powerful that birders could hear the range of voices of the animal kingdom. Though no longer available, SongFinder is being replaced by an app that Elliott and his partner recently developed through their nonprofit, Hear Birds Again.

A seasoned listener, Elliott has learned to adapt so well that his recordings are among the most sought-after interactive tools for

Sit still and you might hear catbirds splashing in the birdbath or posturing in the trees. These funny mimics blend their screechy mews and squawks with phrases from red-winged blackbirds, orioles, and many other species.

people learning about animal vocalizations and natural soundscapes. He has not only recovered the lost words of birds for himself but translated wild languages for the world, producing books and audio compilations celebrating animal voices. He even co-wrote a book on insect songs, despite his natural hearing range shutting out 80 to 90 percent of all insect calls. His classic graduate thesis on chipmunks remains one of the most interesting and fruitful natural history studies of the modern era, gleaning numerous discoveries about the animals' behaviors and the meanings of their calls.

Staying still and quiet, a skill he learned long ago from the works of Ernest Thompson Seton, an early twentieth-century Canadian naturalist, helped Elliott became an interpreter of courtship songs, alarm calls, rain calls, companion chirps, and cries of angst among frogs, birds, and other species. Sitting by a stream near Saranac Lake, New York, he once heard squeaks that he recognized from past adventures: it was a frog in distress. Walking toward the sound, he found a pickerel frog with a leg tangled up in algae. "It was just stuck there," he says, "so I went down and unwrapped its leg and let it go." During another bout of sitting stonelike by the same stream, Elliott heard the sounds of someone coming down the trail. Without moving his head, he recognized the color of a red squirrel. Soon enough, she jumped on his knee with a baby in her mouth, much to Elliott's delight. He knew that squirrels and other mammal moms transport their young to alternate nests when their original homes are disturbed. "So I stayed there for quite a long period of time—over an hour—and it would continue to come back with another youngster, jump up on my knee, and disappear."

In spite of Elliott's severe hearing loss, his experience of the soundscape is much richer than most people's. Rather than learning to listen, our culture has collectively cultivated a "learned deafness"—a phrase introduced by Kurt Fristrup, a retired National Park Service scientist and cofounder of Colorado State University's Sound and Light Ecology Team. Chronic exposure to jet engines, vehicle traffic, industrial machinery, and jacked-up media streaming through earbuds sparks what Fristrup refers to as "generational amnesia," inuring people to the losses. And it's only going to get worse, according to NPS estimates that noise pollution doubles every thirty years, growing faster than the US population.

Seeing canopy-dwelling orioles is a rare treat; the sound identification tool of the Merlin Bird ID app, created by the Cornell Lab of Ornithology, alerts us to their presence and helps us learn their songs.

For those living in areas where noise is more prevalent than natural sounds, "it's terrifying going to places that are quiet," says Francis. "They can hear all these things that they've never heard before: animals rustling in the bushes, distant sounds of things....A real strong sense of place develops what we think should be 'normal' in terms of our sensory environments."

Our perceived human-made comfort zones don't always equate to good health. In addition to hearing loss, our own physiological responses to noise include increased risk for cardiovascular disease, depression, diabetes, sleeplessness, and cognitive impairment. Yet until recently, noise pollution has taken a back seat to other environmental issues, largely because we make decisions with our eyes while tuning out what Les Blomberg calls "audible trash." "Noise is to the soundscape as litter is to the landscape," says the founder of the non-profit Noise Pollution Clearinghouse, based in Montpelier, Vermont. "If we could see noise, it would be McDonald's wrappers thrown out of the car all the way down the highway."

Noise is "the sound of the unsustainable," an acoustic accompaniment to more tangible social and environmental injustices, noted Garret Keizer in *The Unwanted Sound of Everything We Want*. The same roads that slice open wounds through habitat across the continent, carrying noisy vehicles that run over billions of animals each year, have also decimated once-thriving Black and Latino communities since the launch of the US federal highway program in the 1950s. And the same gas-powered leaf blowers that blast away wildlife habitat also acoustically invade the walls of human homes and can permanently damage the hearing of landscape workers within a matter of hours. "The cant that goes with noise, and with every imperial project that behaves like noise," noted Keizer, "is always about 'multiple use,' live and let live. But loud noise does not live and let live." There's a reason noise is used as a weapon of torture against both people and animals; recently I was appalled to find a paper describing an attempt to evict a bobcat mom and her kits from under a deck by blasting a leaf blower at them for three days as a form of "humane harassment." It didn't accomplish the job, but it may have had untold mental and physiological consequences for both the animals and the human neighbors, whose complaints ended the ill-conceived operation.

The low-frequency rumble of anthropogenic noise travels far and can dramatically reduce the distances over which humans and wildlife naturally hear. An increase of even a modest-sounding three decibels can decrease "listening area" by 50 percent, noted Francis and his colleagues in a paper on acoustic environments. "What we're dealing with acoustically in a lot of urban areas is like navigating across a massive landscape in a really dense fog," says Francis, "where you can only see ten meters at a time or so and you're just slowly stumbling around. It's hard to find your destinations. It's hard to find resources that you need when you can only survey that much of an area at a given point."

When the acoustic fog disappeared along with the more visible fog of air in the early days of the COVID-19 pandemic, both people and animals could hear themselves—and each other—talk again. While humans beat a hasty retreat during that short-lived "anthropause," deer, foxes, and alligators took advantage of newly emptied lands, and birds reclaimed the skies above. Many birds expanded their range across the United States and Canada when they no longer needed to avoid the din and danger of roads. They also sang their hearts out. Near the Golden Gate Bridge in San Francisco, white-crowned sparrows even revived low-frequency notes not recorded since 1969, the year of Woodstock and moonwalks.

People were able to hear four times more birds than usual, including some from twice as far away, even when the birds were actually quieter. Adapting to our muted presence, San Francisco's white-crowned sparrows turned down the volume too, adjusting their voices when traffic noise dipped to levels not seen since the mid-1950s. "It turned out they were virtually shouting all the time before with all

Even though birds sang more quietly during the early days of the COVID-19 pandemic, people could hear them from much greater distances than they had before.

the traffic," says David Luther, an associate professor of biology at George Mason University. Released from competition with abundant low-pitch, high-energy noise, the birds could be heard—and so they sang more softly, in a wider bandwidth, with both low notes and high. Urban breeding territories are usually three times louder than those in rural Marin County, but city noise dropped so dramatically during the pandemic that the sound profiles converged. In short, the shutdown was responsible for "effectively reversing more than a half-century rise in noise pollution," noted Luther and his coauthors in the *Science* paper "Singing in a Silent Spring."

Birds can even take the weekend off from the daily grind of commuter traffic, relaxing into their natural songs as noise dissipates. For thirty-six hours a week, when a heavily traveled Washington, DC, commuter road in Rock Creek Park closes to vehicles, Eastern wood pewees sing at much lower frequencies. Teaming up with the National Park Service to record the differences, Luther and then–graduate student Kate Gentry also found that pewees had broader bandwidth and longer songs during quiet periods. "It took me aback at first," he says, "but when I think about it more, we can change our speech, our inflections, our volume…and it makes sense that other animals can too."

The birds' resilience gives Luther hope that we can help them and ourselves. But we have to be willing to adapt too, investing in quieter cars and road surfaces, noise-buffering tree plantings, substitutes for gas-powered machinery, and, most of all, an attitude adjustment. Many thought experiments have explored what the world would be like without us, and the anthropause gave us a real-time glimpse of nature's ability to recover when humans stop making such a racket. But we don't have to vanish from the scene to make it more peaceful

This chipmunk
was busy covering
her burrow entrance
when I accidentally
scared her. She trilled
as she ran away and
leapt to the safety
of the retaining wall.

for our fellow earthlings. Inspired by Elliott's work to expand his listening range despite his impaired hearing, I'm searching for ways to broaden my own aural perceptions—and to limit my disruptions of others' ability to tune in to their ancestral songs.

Trills, Thrills, and Deception: Decoding Hidden Messages

To the shy chipmunk living under the deck, I probably cut a terrifying figure. Barreling around the corner with an orange wheelbarrow full of wood chips one afternoon, laughing riotously through my earbuds while chatting on my phone with a friend, I'm lost in the moment. It's only when I hear sudden high-pitched trills that I look up and see the chippie's petrified face looking back at me from the patio, just before she dashes for the safety of the retaining wall.

I've been watching her from afar for weeks, fascinated by the shifting sands of her daily routines near the deck post, where she's become an expert at clandestinely emerging from her hole and then covering up her tracks with loose, dry soil. It pains me to think of how I've thoughtlessly invaded her space. When Diane Ackerman wrote in *A Natural History of the Senses* that our tools make us "a kind of sensory predator that natural selection never meant us to be," she was talking about the new sound detectors, microscopes, and other technology that allowed us to hear and peer into worlds we would never otherwise experience. Thirty years later, our pocket-size devices do the opposite, compelling us to tune out other lives while babbling distractedly into the ether. More than sensory predators, we've become sensory obliterators.

As I watch the chipmunk trilling, I realize that she is likely trying to talk to her own extended family, alerting them to this new, ungainly hazard. Her voice is quiet and high-pitched, but on this particular afternoon, my rumbling wheelbarrow is her only competition. Chipmunks make several types of alarm calls, and the trill that my inattention inspired is a startle response used more often by females, says Carolyn Mahan, a Penn State biology professor. When it's time to leave the nest, males disperse farther, and females stay closer to home. Mothers sometimes even aggressively expand nearby territories for their daughters and chase their sons away. A given area can contain many relatives, so by trilling near their burrows, females are helping a sister out. "We think it's a signal to other kin that might be in the area that there's a predator, something dangerous nearby," says Mahan.

Chipmunks chirp—a "chip chip chip" sound—in response to terrestrial predators. They cluck more slowly for aerial predators, making a sound that Seton, the early twentieth-century naturalist, compared to horse hooves hitting pavement. Low-frequency clucking sounds carry far and wide and can even launch a chorus of chipmunks across the forest. "The chirps and clucks probably serve the same purpose," says Mahan. "We think those are both messages to the predator that 'I know you're there; I've detected you. You're not going to surprise me, so go hunt elsewhere.'"

It would be reasonable to assume that the motivations of clucking chipmunks have long been known to Indigenous peoples with deep knowledge of natural signals and cues, but it remained a mystery in the scientific literature until Elliott spent several years studying the animals in the Adirondacks of New York State. It was sometimes hard to spot birds flying above in his forested study area, but eventually he noticed a trend: the chipmunks were sounding off at the same time that hawks flew overhead. "It passes like a wave, initiated by one that saw a hawk or thought they saw a hawk," he says. Whether the other chipmunks saw the hawk themselves or just heard their fellow chippies firing up the alarm system didn't seem to matter; they joined right in. "It was contagious. Chipmunks would start doing the clucking along the path of the hawk and would keep going for quite a while and then finally die out."

Often perched on a log, frozen in position, they looked so still it wouldn't be possible to see the tiny movements of their throats without binoculars, says Elliott, who has since recorded a whole hillside of chipmunks clucking in New York's Shindagin Hollow State Forest. Even though they're generally solitary in their foraging activities and living spaces, their cooperative alarm systems provide advantages to the whole group. "So if a chipmunk knows the hawk is there, it's not really in any danger because they're agile," says Elliott. "They have holes; they know where to go."

Many animals must be quiet in the presence of predators, navigating a tricky balancing act between wooing mates and drawing attention from the wrong crowd. In forested areas, the túngara frogs of Central America have to remain vigilant for bats who would eat them and midges who would bite them. Where predators and parasites are scarcer, as they generally are in urban areas, the males step up their game, singing faster and adding more embellishments—complex love songs that females prefer. When relocated to forests, the urban frogs dampen their bravado accordingly to avoid being eaten. "It really shows where males are in a tug-of-war between what females want," says Cy Mott, an associate professor of biology at Eastern Kentucky University, "and what other selective pressure is put on them, like predation."

Eavesdropping is common among multilinguist animals, as when nuthatches tune in to nuanced chickadee alarm calls to assess owl threats, squirrels listen to blue jays to evaluate the safety of nut-caching sites, and groundhogs heed the alarm calls of crows. Making the study of the wild soundscape even more complicated, some animals exploit these tendencies, harnessing sound for deceptive purposes and issuing what ecologists call "dishonest signals." Blue jays mimic hawk calls, a behavior likely intended to scare other species away from food or nests. Similarly, at least two Amazon species—the bluish-slate antshrike and the white-winged shrike-tanager—have been seen faking out their neighbors. Issuing warning calls normally reserved for signaling the presence of hawks, they can create false alarms that send other birds packing and thus reduce competition for insect treats. It's likely that many more animals "cry wolf," as one researcher put it, repurposing trusted signals to gain an advantage.

Keeping an ear out for male competitors, animals can harness both sound and silence to potentially make up for apparent inadequacies. Small green frogs, like some of my friends in the pond, have been shown to deepen their voices by emitting lower-frequency pitches in response to the calls of larger males—possibly making themselves sound bigger and bolder than they really are. But being the loudest doesn't always get animals what they want. "Satellite males" of some species, including a number of tree frogs, use the opposite strategy, posing as silent types and following around a crooning male who is bigger, older, or in better condition. If they're lucky, these hangers-on

The love songs of seventeen-year cicadas often result in successful unions, but sometimes a fungus takes over auditory communications to spread its own spores.

can intercept an impending romantic encounter at the last moment, making off with the female and leaving the hardworking songster in the dust.

Bats initiate moments of silence too, and we've only recently begun to understand why. Scientists once thought that the flying mammals relied exclusively on echolocation to navigate and forage, emitting high-frequency sound pulses that bounce off objects and echo back to their ears. But bats also use other senses, notably vision, to make their way through the night. Recent research suggests that they know when it's best to avoid speaking up: when flying behind another bat, a big brown bat often stops vocalizing to prevent sonar jamming, but he still finds his way through space, likely by listening in on the leading bat's calls. Hoary bats switch back and forth between high-intensity echolocation and silence or "micro calls," presumably to stay under the radar of other males during mating season.

Adding to the already crowded airwaves are insects who know how to fight back. Many have ears that can detect the high-frequency sounds of bats zeroing in on them. Among the most studied are tiger moth species that can produce ultrasonic clicks, which are thought to startle the bats, interfere with their echolocation, or serve as a poison warning label that alerts the bats to their plant-derived toxicity. Firefly species found in Vietnam and Israel have recently been shown to use such "musical armor," as researcher Ksenia Krivoruchko calls it; their flashing behaviors already warn predators of their unpalatability, but clicking at a frequency that bats can hear may add another layer of defense.

Clicking is an honest signal among cicadas—until it's not. Females respond to male songs by flipping their wings and emitting a quiet sound that approximates the snapping of human fingers, a lure that males find irresistible. But for those seventeen-year cicadas unlucky enough to be infected with a fungus called *Massospora cicadina*, the system falls apart. Even though the fungus destroys their genitals, the hijacked cicadas go into sexual overdrive, spreading the pathogen with abandon. Some infected males even click like females, attracting other males with the promise of a good time but passing along the spores instead.

The male toads who gather for their springtime orgies near our pond and patio are more truthful with each other, bleeping short, squeaky trills that say, "You're wasting your time!" In the heat of the

American toads take a brief respite under our deck from their chaotic "mating balls."

As these toads mated in our pond, they blinked their eyes simultaneously every ten seconds or so while the rest of the toads continued to call.

A wood frog who lost out on the action watches a mating pair leap away.

moment, the toads are desperate to mate and not very discriminating, but these "release calls" let other males know they've got the wrong toad. "It's a really short, energetically cheap call to make," says Mott, "because you want to dedicate your time and your energy to the big, impressive trill calls that impress the females."

The evolutionary ingenuity of males trying to stand out in the sonic crowd certainly is a bit dazzling, at least to this human female. Breeding choruses aren't just timed to take advantage of acoustic niches across species, with different types of frogs singing at different frequencies. As they rise from their winter sleep, individual males within a species also alternate calling times, their way of showing their unique flair while bellying up to the singles bar. Without such coordination, females wouldn't be able to discern one potential suitor from another. "You'd just get a whole bunch of individuals all saying 'Hey!' at the same time," says Mott. "You have two or three individuals that might overlap a little, but every time there's a little space, another individual tries to get their call in. And that's beneficial for the female too because she can make an accurate assessment of which calls are the longest and the deepest."

Watching a frog or toad "mating ball" reveals how fierce the vocal competition can be. One day by the ponds, enjoying the ducklike blurts of wood frogs heralding the coming of spring, I see a soap-opera drama play out on the rocks. After frantically piling all over each other to try to get to a female, swimming and splashing their way around the pond, the males finally break apart and let a newly joined couple hop up to the side. As the large female leads the way through the leaves toward two smaller tub ponds, carrying her mate on top, another forlorn-looking frog pulls up to the edge. He spreads his toes out on a stone, peers over the side, and watches the newly-weds ride off into the sunset. Where did he go wrong? Maybe he wasn't loud enough or fast enough, or maybe he should have arrived sooner to the party. Whatever the reason for his lack of luck in love, he appears to be at a loss for words even as his many other rivals keep right on clucking, looking every bit as wistful as a human pining for the one who got away.

After our startling encounter, the shy chipmunk eludes me for a while. We finally meet again when I emerge from the pathway to the pond, but this time we're both quiet. She dives under the rocks, leaving all the trilling and clucking to the frogs and toads. What does she think of the songs they sing? Does she understand the lyrics? Do they in turn pay attention to her clucked warnings whenever a hawk is drawing near?

Changing Their Tunes: The Struggle to Be Heard

The natural soundscape is far from silent, filled with rushing rivers, crashing waterfalls, gusty winds, and grasshoppers and crickets stridulating away. Animals have always contended with finding their voices in the glorious messiness of nature, but they've had many thousands of years to learn how to fit in.

Some highly vocal species are quite creative, literally getting a leg up on the competition by appealing to other senses. To augment the effectiveness of their peeps, squeals, and courtship calls, torrent frogs living along fast-flowing streams in the Amazon wave their arms, shake their feet, bob and snake their heads, and tremble their toes.

It's not unlike when someone needs to grab the attention of a person who can't hear well; during my presentations, I don't expect audience members to start shaking their booties if they have a question, but it helps if they raise their hands or stand up so I can pinpoint where they are.

Using their surroundings strategically, tree crickets have an elegant solution for keeping up with their larger, loudmouth competitors: males eat holes in leaves, stick their heads through them, and chirp two to three times louder through their DIY megaphones than they otherwise would be able to. Some amphibians have figured out how to commandeer human-made structures to similar advantage; Mientien tree frogs use the urban canyons of storm drains to amplify and draw out their songs. Such behaviors are probably present in many species but have yet to be studied. In North America, some gray tree frogs inhabit both the natural canopy and human-built metal gutters, raising the question: Are they manipulating their surroundings into their own personal sound system?

It's possible, says Mott. Their preference for humid locations like watery cavities in trees may steer them to human-made spots that approximate those environments, and their accidental success could eventually influence future generations. "Natural selection picks the winners and losers, and so they might not know that they're amplifying their call, but if it brings more females to them—and if that's in any way a heritable trait—then they're going to have offspring that maybe pick those kinds of locations too."

The question of how quickly organisms can adjust to novel noises in human-dominated environments is behind an ever-growing body of research exploring our impacts on the soundscape.

Communications in the wild are so complex that scientists have barely begun to decode them, let alone even partially quantify the consequences of disruption. Creatures we tend to think of as quiet are often not so shy and retiring after all; they're just responding to interference in ways that are hard for our human ears to detect. When disturbed, walnut sphinx moth caterpillars hiss and Abbott's sphinx moth caterpillars unleash mouse-like squeaks. Plants under duress due to drought or physical injury emit ultrasonic sounds. They can also "hear" by sensing the vibrations of airborne sound waves; one study showed that thale cress amps up production of defensive compounds when exposed to recordings of a caterpillar chewing. Flowers harness natural sound for positive pursuits, tuning in to the buzz of pollinators to increase production; researchers in Israel found that in the presence of bees' wingbeats, a primrose species was even able to sweeten its nectar. Like animals, plants can suffer in the presence of human-made noise; a recent study in Iran showed elevated levels of stress hormones and stunted growth in marigolds and salvias forced to grow next to a busy highway.

Depending on the species, animals might change the amplitude, timing, duration, and pitch of their sounds to get their points across. Frogs with low voices, like green frogs and bull frogs, have been observed saving their breath until the din dies down. Some other frogs, as well as mammals and birds, have been found to sing and call at higher frequencies in the midst of noise. Birds in urban environments also wake up earlier to start their dawn chorus, possibly to beat rush-hour traffic. In California, long-term studies of white-crowned sparrows have found that city birds are fast talkers, with more rapid trills and shorter whistles than those of their rural counterparts. But they have a narrower range than their country cousins. "It's hard to

White-crowned sparrows living in the city sing in a narrower range of pitch than their counterparts in more rural areas, but they trill more rapidly.

sing fast with a wide bandwidth," explains Jennifer Phillips, who rode her bike around San Francisco to record sparrows during the pandemic for the "Silent Spring" study.

Given a choice, female white-crowned sparrows prefer males who combine broad vocal ranges with speed, qualities that also impress male competitors. "It could be like some bodybuilder flexing in the gym," says Luther. "It's like a signal saying, 'I'm better, I can do more, I'm tougher, don't mess with me' to the others of the same sex. And then to the opposite sex, it's saying, 'Yeah, I am great, you gotta come over and get some of this because I'm in good shape.'"

For males in cities, there may be no point in wasting time on the lower notes if they'll only end up lost in the grumble and grind of human industry and transportation, so they compensate in other ways. "That's the vocal performance trade-off," says Phillips, now an assistant professor of biology at Texas A&M University-San Antonio. "You don't need to sing a wide bandwidth if no one can hear you. So you can reduce your energy in terms of bandwidth and instead spend your energy performing a faster trill rate. And you're still getting that sexier song."

Songbirds learn to sing in their formative first few months by listening to those around them. Acoustic adaptation theory posits that, over time, different populations develop slightly different dialects that will be heard in their given habitats. "What we thought about these birds was that once they crystallized their song, it's crystallized for life," says Phillips.

But the cosmopolitan white-crowned sparrows added a new wrinkle by showing some flexibility in the range of their complex notes. Their standard song starts with a whistled alert along the lines of

"Hey, I'm over here," Phillips explains. The complex notes that follow are individual trademarks: "My name is Bob." After that comes the trill: "And this is how good I am."

"And so the part that they're kind of changing plastically is the way they say their name—basically, those complex notes: 'I'm Bob,'" Phillips says in a deep voice. "So they might say"—(and at this, Phillips's voice goes up several octaves)—"'I'm Bob!' if it's noisy out so maybe you can hear them better."

How well Bob the white-crowned sparrow's potential mates and competitors in the city can hear his higher-frequency calls is still an open question that scientists are actively exploring; studies of other birds have shown weakened territorial response in the presence of anthropogenic noise. But when the songs do reach the sparrows' ears, they appear to get the message loud and clear. Male birds treat vocal incursion as a "home invasion," says Luther, and white-crowned sparrows get so triggered that they wave their wings as if they are making tight fists, "like they almost can't get the words out." Testing both sparrow and cardinal responses in loud areas, Luther and his colleagues found that songs adjusted to rise above the din elicited the strongest response, suggesting that intruders with altered voices were still deemed noteworthy competitors.

Even if animals appear to be adjusting, they may suffer other negative effects on their overall health and fitness. Urban white-crowned sparrows have higher survival rates than their country counterparts, but they also have poorer body conditions. Seemingly positive outcomes for a given species may be more equivocal at second glance. Phillips, Francis, and graduate student Josh Willems found that pinyon mice—a southwestern species native to pinyon-juniper forests and other arid and semiarid habitats—actually gravitate toward areas near loud gas compressors. The sound likely obscures their activities and helps them hide from hawks and snakes, but the mice in noisy areas are also in worse body condition. "So there is a trade-off. You're not getting eaten, but you're kind of more stressed out and still losing that body mass," says Phillips. "It's like humans: if you have a constant level of noise, you might get used to it and not think it's a big deal, but if you actually looked at your stress hormone levels, they're probably more elevated than someone who lives in a totally quiet area."

In the struggle to hear and be heard, maybe we're all much more a product of our environment than we've realized. Even humans with normal hearing lose bits of conversation that are drowned out by noise. Adapting to and compensating for loud modernity is harder than most people realize, whether they've already been deafened by noise or not. After a lifetime of looking for my own acoustic niche, I wonder if I'm a little like the rural bird, a little like the urban bird, and maybe even a little like my frog friends—a hybrid of all, my voice a vaguely southern drawl of slower trills set into a narrower urban bandwidth that comes not from talking over noise but trying to listen and speak up in the spaces between.

Road Rage: Stress and Vigilance

The cars that zoom down our two-lane rural road going twice the twenty-five-mile-per-hour speed limit hit owls, box turtles, deer, cats, butterflies, and other animals, most of whom are too mangled to

Monarch caterpillars now eat milkweed and make their chrysalises away from the roadside in our habitat, after I moved the plants to reduce their stress.

save. These impacts of human carelessness are direct, unnecessary, and infuriating in their callous disregard for life. But while inspecting our milkweed by the front walking path one day, I notice a more hidden consequence. On the underside of a leaf, a monarch caterpillar scrunches her body, visibly flinching and raising her head each time a self-appointed race car driver flies past.

It turns out I'm not the only one who's observed this behavior. Around the same time, a University of Georgia researcher published a study confirming the caterpillars' discomfort. By placing them under a microscope and watching for movements of their "hearts"—long vessels along the caterpillars' backs that pump hemolymph, or insect blood—research scientist Andy Davis found that simulated traffic noise causes elevated heart rates indicative of stress.

Larvae raised amid the noise were also aggressive, more likely to curl into a defensive ball when handled, and prone to lashing out at Davis's student helpers. "We were kind of shocked that the monarch caterpillars bit us," says Davis, whose wife also studies the butterflies. "We've probably handled thousands of monarch caterpillars, and we'd never been bitten by one." The caterpillars were also thrashing around, a very unusual response to being handled. In short, they had road rage: "They were literally stressed from the noise. Whenever animals get stressed, there is always a corresponding change in behavior where they get more aggressive."

After a week, the monarchs' heart rates lowered again, but that didn't mean they were OK, says Davis. A certain amount of stress is important to animals' survival, giving them a chance to react to dangerous situations. But chronic exposure can cause them to lose that ability. "My study raised this possibility that maybe being stressed so often by the noise is actually damaging their physiology in some way," Davis says. "And we also know from animal studies that when animals are stressed repeatedly at a young stage—like butterfly caterpillars—[they] carry that stress over into their adult life. Even humans do this. People that grow up in a stressful environment become poorly adapted to dealing with regular stressors."

More mobile animals can choose between fight and flight. In a study of mixed-species flocks of birds in the congested suburbs of northern Virginia, Luther and his students found that cardinals, Carolina wrens, and Carolina chickadees were more likely to fly away from locations rife with traffic noise than from quieter places. During the winter, these birds join forces with downy woodpeckers and other species, foraging and traveling together to increase their chances of finding food and avoiding predation. Brash tufted titmice act as sentinels, warning the flock of danger and even changing the notes and duration of their alarm calls to indicate which type of predator is lurking. In the presence of recorded titmice warning calls in congested areas, the birds stopped foraging more quickly, didn't spend as much time eating, and flew faster into hiding places, presumably because they knew the traffic noise could hamper their ability to effectively monitor their surroundings.

Increased vigilance is a fairly common response in vertebrates who use hearing as a universal passive surveillance system. While vision is more directional, we rely on hearing to survey the environment for dangers or opportunities without actually focusing our attention on the task. "When that modality is compromised in some way, a lot of different species will reliably start using other senses, especially for threat detection," says Francis. "So we know that in a lot of birds, with increases in sound level they spend a lot more time scanning, visually looking around for threats."

Every reaction can ripple out indefinitely. When researchers discovered ground squirrels' increased vigilance around wind turbines, they predicted diminished food for squirrel predators like golden eagles and reduced housing for inhabitants of squirrel-dug burrows like tiger salamanders and burrowing owls. Noise near prairie dogs, whose colonies and burrows provide shelter and food for a wide range of other species, threatens to lead to similar displacement. Among the scant noise pollution studies involving wild mammals, research in Colorado found that the sounds of traffic reduced prairie dogs' foraging and resting times and diminished their social behaviors, sparked significantly more vigilance, and resulted in fewer individuals going aboveground. Long-term, widespread extermination programs, combined with the flea-borne bacterial disease sylvatic plague and urban development, have already pushed prairie-dog colonies into isolated pockets of habitat close to humans. Adaptable as these gregarious, talkative animals are, they may be no match for the level of land fragmentation and disturbance that living near our species inflicts upon them.

Just as prey animals need to work harder to escape becoming food when they can't hear predators well, predators who rely on sound to find their meals are affected when the volume gets too high. Experiments in Japan and the United States have shown that the noise produced by traffic and natural gas compressors reduces owls' chances of finding prey. Even the smallest of creatures, like parasitoids, may suffer when their soundscape is disrupted. To find food for their young, female tachinid flies known as *Ormia ochracea* use their exceptional directional hearing to home in on the mating calls of field crickets; the flies then deposit larvae on and around the crickets, and those larvae feed on the crickets from the inside—and kill them— before emerging to pupate. But Phillips and her colleagues found that increased background noise reduces the presence of the tachinid flies significantly, potentially altering this host-parasitoid relationship.

While that might sound like good news for crickets and the larger animals who rely on those crickets for food, it could spell trouble for plants that suddenly have more cricket mouths to feed or for predators of flies faced with diminished food supplies. "There can be a lot of cascading consequences to a certain level of noise pollution that can be difficult to see at first glance," notes Phillips, "and it is easy to write off noise pollution if you don't have studies that are actually documenting this type of thing."

Exploring these more hidden effects at the Rattlesnake Canyon Habitat Management Area in New Mexico, Francis, Phillips, and

Wolf spiders carry their young on their back until the spiderlings are ready to disperse. Sensitive to vibrations, they've been found to avoid noisy areas.

other scientists found that noise can change the composition of avian, insect, and plant communities. Covered in pinyon-juniper woodlands and sagebrush grasslands, the area includes both quiet patches and those where the soundscape is contaminated by compressors used for extraction by natural gas companies. While loud, the sound isn't unusually so when compared with anthropogenic noise levels in other areas of the country.

Because of the site's location, remote from human activity, researchers can isolate the effects of noise with few confounding variables. They've documented the disappearance of arthropods in the loud areas, including dramatic decreases in abundance of wolf spiders, velvet ants, froghoppers, grasshoppers, and several species of crickets. They've shown that many birds avoid noise altogether, resulting in "a complete loss of one-third of the species that nest in these areas," notes Francis. They've observed that some insects and birds, such as black-chinned hummingbirds and Western bluebirds, actually nest in greater numbers near the noise, possibly using it as a shield to mask their sounds from predators. But what's gained in protection may be lost in quality of life and overall health, as with Davis's caterpillars. The researchers discovered strong physiological evidence that females and chicks of several different species nesting at the site experience noise-induced stress.

Among the birds who avoid the noisy spots altogether are scrub jays, important seed dispersers of pinyon pines. More than a decade ago, when Francis and his colleagues quantified the number of seedlings that had sprouted in quiet plots versus those containing natural gas compressors, the differences were dramatic: four times fewer pines grew in the noisy plots. Since then, some of the compressors have gone silent, reopening a sensory niche for the possible return of the birds and the trees they inadvertently plant as they bury their stash. But even after the quiet resumed, the woodlands have not recovered, meaning that jays are still staying away.

Seedling recruitment of Utah junipers also plummeted in noisy plots, where seven times fewer of them sprouted. Noise changed the abundance of different shrubs and wildflowers too, altering the composition of the plant communities. The findings raise questions about how many other animals are drawn to the noise and how many are pushed away. Do bees and other pollinators who communicate acoustically avoid these areas and thus depress the pollination of many species? Do mice who eat more pine seeds near noise also feed in appreciable numbers on seeds of other plants? Are other browsing mammals disproportionately attracted to noisy plots?

"One of our biggest challenges right now is we mainly are still kind of stuck in thinking about the direct effects of sound, and we've kind of scratched the surface in New Mexico of thinking about how animals or even plants are impacted indirectly," says Francis. "But these webs are pretty large in these noise-exposed areas across the world....A species you might not even expect—that doesn't even have ears or any way of hearing—may be changing in abundance because of some other species that you're not even focusing on."

Creating a Real Birdland

"What news have you brought from your journey?" I want to ask the pine siskins when they touch down in the tulip trees in October. But I don't dare move for fear of sending these adventurous little finches away. My own plans for crossing the continent to see loved ones have been scrapped this year, so I feel lucky to host these weary wild travelers, who've flown in all the way from Canada to sample American menus. Dozens descend and alight at once, drinking from the pond, climbing the trees, and poking around for seeds, sap, and insects.

The coming weeks will bring reports of massive numbers of pine siskins, evening grosbeaks, and other birds of the boreal forest touching down on our more southerly soil, trees, and feeders. Irruptions

A pine siskin took a break from the frenzy at our pond one fall, when dozens descended and chattered away softly as they sipped water and bathed.

occur periodically and unpredictably, but it won't be long before scientists suggest what spurred this one: boreal birds had a productive spring during the early days of the pandemic, when Canadian foresters weren't able to spray as much pesticide as they normally do. Plenty of baby food—in the form of spruce budworms—meant plenty of healthy chicks. But by autumn, the trees are producing fewer seeds and nuts than usual, and bounty has given way to scarcity. Boom and bust years are a natural occurrence, with trees varying their output over time, but the failed crop is bad timing for the birds.

The confluence of events is an unanticipated outcome of the global lockdowns. By attempting to prevent "super-spreaders" of the novel coronavirus, humans created circumstances that led to these "super-flights" of birds on the move.

A pair of pine siskins perch on a branch beyond the pond, leaning on each other as the others swirl about in constant motion. *Welcome to the B&B,* I think. *Please make yourselves at home!* But these gregarious songbirds need no invitation. Their constant chatter is soft around the edges but insistent, a particularly joyful-sounding example of a "companion call" or "contact call"—the birds' way of keeping in touch. "They're generally short-range calls," says Luther, "like if you're almost in the same room with somebody and just kind of talking: *Hey, I'm here! I found some food! I got this! What are you doing later?*" Listening to their conversation reminds me of a favorite storybook conversation, when Piglet whispers Pooh's name, hears "Yes, Piglet?" and responds, "Oh nothing, I was just making sure of you." The birds' twitters sound like the same quiet reassurances, punctuated occasionally by a call reminiscent of zipping up a tent for the night. Some birders call it the "watch-winding" note, presumably recalling old-school wristwatches; others liken the sound to tearing a paper slowly in two. Our sensory experiences are laden with our own memories, filtered through the known world to make sense of the unknown.

Many of these quieter communications are less studied, usually because they aren't considered as urgent or important as songs and calls directly associated with breeding and reproduction. My initial journey in learning more about nature's musical languages led me to quite a few books and other references claiming that female birds don't sing. They're not calling for mates or defending territories, the writers reasoned, so why would they need to find their voices? We now know otherwise, thanks in part to the growing number of women in ornithology. Female singing is most common in the tropics, where paired birds of some species hold and defend territory year-round together.

Only a few in North America, like cardinals, are thought to pipe up. But I wonder if one day we'll find that we just haven't listened enough yet. Maybe we'll even redefine what qualifies as "song." Back in their northern breeding grounds next summer, the females of my pine siskin flock won't be shy about speaking up for what they need, quietly beckoning males to mate "by uttering soft calls while bowing and fluttering tail and wing feather," as the Cornell Lab of Ornithology describes their sweet interactions. "The female solicits feeding from the male with a low twittering call that carries well through the trees."

Low-frequency calls travel farther through a forest, and some birds' voices are well adapted to living and communicating under that dense canopy. But what works in a forest is what makes it even harder for animals to be heard against a backdrop of noise emitted at similar pitches. I'm grateful the pine siskins have decided to visit during a brief reprieve from the chainsaw of my neighbor, who tends to spend the hour between the end of his workday and dinner cutting things down. But I cringe in anticipation of his postprandial return, which may drown out these beautiful voices.

Like physical illness, noise falls into two general categories: chronic and episodic. Noise pollution research has typically focused on the chronic variety, partly because it's easier to study and partly because it's so ubiquitous; most places in the United States are less than a mile from a road. As noise from other sources grows in volume and duration, with more homeowners hiring landscaping companies that deploy large crews of mower cowboys and leaf-blowing soldiers with machines strapped to their backs, the question becomes: At what point does the episodic become chronic, adding yet another layer of aural harm?

Little to no research exists on the effects of acute landscaping noises on our wild neighbors. But as Davis notes, if the occasional passing car emitting a seventy-five-decibel sound stresses out a monarch caterpillar, "It really makes you think: How many other stressors are we exposing these caterpillars to in our daily lives?"

My neighbor's landscaping crew blasting one-hundred-plus-decibel gas-powered leaf blowers at close range along our fence line could be just as damaging, especially when the noise travels from house to house all day. "It's not like it's just a gunshot going very quickly and then gone, which we might expect to cause these really strong startle responses, and it may take a little while for animals to reset their behavior," says Francis, who hears leaf blowers the entire length of his bike ride to work in San Luis Obispo. "It's common enough with weed whackers or leaf blowers that it goes for five, ten minutes, and those can be long enough durations where it's really disrupting what can be a critical communication time for a lot of songbirds. Most males are engaging in their mate attraction and territorial defense types of behaviors in the morning."

While the effects of landscaping noise on wildlife remains unquantified, we know enough about animals' reactions to other intermittent noise to draw some general inferences. Researchers who've studied the responses of elk, bison, wolves, and foxes to snowmobiles report elevated stress levels, escape behaviors, and increased energy expenditures.

It's not a bad hair day; this Carolina wren just emerged from the birdbath salon. When not beautifying himself, he wakes us up at the crack of dawn with his "teakettle! teakettle! teakettle!" call.

Even quick aircraft flyovers can be devastating: once, when Krause was recording a chorus of rare spadefoot toads disrupted by a military jet, it took the doomed toads forty-five minutes to sync back up, and by then it was too late. The collective song had provided strength in numbers, but the breakdown into scattered parts invited a coyote and great horned owl to quickly find and eat the individuals. In a recent laboratory study, a low-frequency fire alarm test—a routine lab noise—found that brief exposure interfered with zebra finch behaviors for at least fifteen minutes, potentially compromising their welfare.

After a few days of finding sanctuary in our little woodlands, the pine siskin flock moves on. Wherever they end up, I hope it's quiet.

Migratory birds are avoiding noisy areas now, according to a recent global analysis. But what about the animals who must stay, with no other home to go to? Though wild birds can technically fly away, that's not an option for nesting parents who can't leave their young. I can afford noise-canceling headphones, which help me work while neighbors saw down trees along the road and replace them with "This is Birdland" decorative flags to celebrate the Baltimore Orioles baseball team. My white-noise machine helps me sleep on nights when the highway is loud. If it becomes too unbearable, I can move. But many others, both human and nonhuman, don't have that choice. It is for them that I stay, nurturing a resistance to the no-man's-lands—or, perhaps more accurately, the only-man's-lands.

Just as noise begets noise, the songs of birds, frogs, crickets, and grasshoppers can build on themselves too, drawing more wildlife back home. Together with a smattering of neighbors who also have started to hear the calls of the wild and nurture habitat for them, we will try to turn this community into a real birdland—and a land for chipmunks, spiders, bees, trees, and peace-loving people too.

CHAPTER 3

The Tastescape

Please don't eat me, or at least not all of me.

—every plant and animal on Earth

Sulphur butterflies are sipping nectar from blue waxweed flowers while green-eyed wasps pick over the grocery aisles of pink swamp milkweed. Syrphid flies and bumblebees scramble across the yellow smooth sumac blossoms to sample the latest inventory. Yellow-bellied sapsuckers drill holes in the elm, releasing sweetness that hummingbirds and Eastern comma butterflies will later lap up too. Nocturnal gray tree frogs nestle between the deck beams, perhaps dreaming of the slugs and spiders they'll snack on tonight. Green frogs work the day shift to snag passing morsels in the pond. Red-tailed hawks circle over the meadow, putting the squirrels on notice, while a black rat snake drinks from a sidewalk puddle that collected as I filled my watering cans.

Everyone is in their place: the pollinators on the flowers, the frogs and raptors on the prowl, the birds hiding in the bushes. Or are they? Strolling past a dinner-plate-turned-birdbath I just refreshed two hours ago, I notice a diminutive summer azure butterfly busily

A summer azure butterfly took up water for an hour from the birdbath, presumably collecting trace salts.

The salty residue left by my hand on my camera intrigued this Zabulon skipper.

walking back and forth around the edge. Occasionally he takes in fresh water, often excreting liquid at the same time, before circling the rim again. As I watch him over the next hour, a pattern unfolds: after drinking, excreting, and returning to where it's high and dry, he eventually heads to the scene of an excreted droplet, sinks his proboscis into the center, and sucks it back up again.

To this diminutive blue butterfly, the flowers bursting forth all over the gardens hold little allure right now. The birdbath is where it's at: prime beachfront property with a salty private sea lapping at its ceramic orange shoreline. He's taking in not just water but whatever invisible bits of myself I've shed while rinsing out the dish. As far as I'm aware, I've left only fingerprints, but to the butterfly, the residues of my sweat might be a lifeline. And soon enough, word seems to travel fast among the azure's cousins, because that evening as I settle into a chair on the patio with my books and a glass of water, an Eastern-tailed blue butterfly (another tiny, flashy member of the Lycaenidae family) lands on my big toe. My toe is apparently a fabulous roadside attraction for insect travelers; years ago I was reading in the same spot when a dragonfly decided to use it as a lookout tower, zipping off to catch prey and returning repeatedly all afternoon to survey his domain.

The Eastern-tailed blue doesn't fly as far afield, leaving my toe only to probe everything else I've recently touched: one of my flip-flops, all three books on the table, the table itself, and the rim of my drinking glass. For two hours he extends his proboscis onto these surfaces, and though I can't see it with my poor eyesight and standard camera, I assume he's combining small amounts of fluid with traces of my sweat to create an accessible slurry of needed nutrients. When I see a Zabulon skipper engaging in similar behavior a few weeks later, I wonder if I should retrieve my macro lens to capture more detail— but the task would be impossible, as the skipper is actually sitting on the camera itself, extending his proboscis around the strap and the power button.

Animals rely on sodium for a number of physiological processes, including neuromuscular function, fluid regulation, digestion, and excretion. From butterflies and bees to moose and squirrels, they seek natural salt licks to supplement their diets. Some animals take a more drastic approach, like the Mormon crickets indigenous to western rangelands, who solve salt deprivation problems through cannibalism. Others get creative and take advantage of the human-built environment. Even car and machinery parts lure salt-seeking rodents. "Sometimes they're going after a place to feed, to nest, but a lot of times they're just going after the salt that's been left from somebody's hands on the hoses," says Carol Boggs, a biology professor at the University of South Carolina. When her husband was working at the Rocky Mountain Biological Lab in Colorado, marmots repeatedly gnawed the weather recording equipment. "They had to soak the stuff in the hottest hot sauce they could find to keep rodents from chewing on the wires to get the salt that had been left from their hands."

Salt cravings can depend on proximity to the sea. One study found that ants living closer to the coast weren't as attracted to sodium baits as those farther inland, presumably because they'd gotten what they needed from salt-sprayed plants. Inland plants generally have low sodium content, so herbivores often find sodium in nonvegeta-tive sources. Butterflies are known to gather salt and amino acids—a behavior known as "puddling"—from wet sand and gravel, driveways,

My sweaty skin attracts Eastern comma butterflies.

rotting fruit, animal flesh, poop, urine, and sweat. In the Amazon, butterflies have been filmed lapping up turtle tears; in Costa Rica, they've feasted on literal crocodile tears. At the 2021 Australian Open, when a common brown butterfly landed on Naomi Osaka's leg, she gently carried him to the sidelines, but he didn't take the separation well and flew onto her nose. "Butterfly blesses Naomi Osaka," TV outlets gushed. "The butterfly is in love with you," someone tweeted admiringly.

I admit to feeling a similar thrill and kinship when Eastern comma butterflies land on my knee or little glassywing skippers sit on Will's sweaty hand as he winds down from a run around the neighborhood. But clingy butterflies aren't looking for romance, at least not with us. They often have other loves on their minds, and salt collection plays an important role: when mating, male butterflies transfer sodium and other nutrients in a spermatophore, or sperm packet, to females. Over time, all those nuptial gifts can deplete their own resources, so males may puddle again to replenish what they've lost. Older females of some species also puddle, having already passed along much of their supply to their young.

Butterflies dining on human sweat and raccoon poop might not fit the idealized images we hold of our most beloved and glamorous insects. But the tastescape is full of surprises, shaped partly by the things we all leave behind. A bird eats a blueberry at the edge of the woods, flies later to a fence rail, and expels the seed of a new bush whose fruit may eventually land in our mouths. An aphid excretes sugary pee known as "honeydew" onto a stem, and ants lap it up, defending the aphids against predators in exchange for the gift, a kind of "let-me-eat-and-you-won't-be-eaten" peace pact. As I park my car at my favorite restaurant, vultures swoop in for a fine dining experience too—at the dumpsters full of discarded lunches from the pizza joint next door. Inside our homes, insects like silverfish clean up after us, able to feast on skin flakes, fungal spores, animal hairs, paper, rayon, cotton fibers, pollen, sand grains, bacteria, and plant tissue; in his book *Never Home Alone,* ecologist Rob Dunn even cites a report of a silverfish surviving on the dust beneath a wineglass for at least three months.

Wherever we go, we shed parts of ourselves and someone else picks up the pieces. When researchers discovered that insects leave traceable

DNA on flowers, providing a way to track who's visiting a specific plant, they also had to allow for the fact that some DNA showing up in their surveys may have been delivered not by its original owner but by another insect who had picked up the genetic material while foraging. When butterflies are tasting the residue of my fingerprints with the chemoreceptors in their feet, they're leaving their own footprints too, absorbing bits of me while depositing bits of themselves in their wake.

It's hard to tell where other senses end and taste begins. Touch, smell, sound, and sight all play a role in locating food and avoiding becoming food yourself. The tastescape is a sensory feast filled with moments of sweetness: a tired papa cardinal teaches his fledglings to forage among flowerpots while taking frequent breaks to feed them; a mother deer and her fawn reunite in the evenings for a nursing session. But it's also a treacherous place, with the need to feed starting more wars among the plants and animals in one backyard than among people around the world throughout human history. From the gangs of tufted titmice mobbing a black rat snake trying to grab a stealthy meal to the frogs diving under their water lily refuges at the slightest sound of footsteps, animals are in a race for survival. Godspeed to the ant crossing the patio in the pathway of the vibration-sensitive and voracious tiger beetle, to the male bee in the meadow lured by the fake perfume of a predatory beetle larva who will eventually eat all the bee's babies, and to the vegetarian long-horned beetle larvae munching away behind a tree's bark with a woodpecker listening in.

In the battle of the appetites, plants can not only use their own senses to "taste" who's eating them and shore up their defenses as necessary but also offer sweet rewards to a mercenary army of arthropods.

Many species stock extrafloral nectaries to deliver nectar from stems and other parts outside the flower. In exchange for the treat, predatory insects and spiders serve as vigilantes, protecting plants from those who would eat them.

Sometimes plants take a more direct route, eating animals themselves. Everyone knows about the Venus flytrap, and many have heard of the carnivorous pitcher plants and sundews. But a recent discovery has scientists wondering how many more flesh-eating species we may be overlooking. Western false asphodel, *Triantha occidentalis*, is an unassuming killer hiding in plain sight in urban areas of the Pacific Northwest. By secreting the enzyme phosphatase along its sticky stems, the white-blooming wildflower can directly digest tiny insects like midges and obtain significant amounts of nitrogen. In a paper about the plant, botanist Qianshi Lin and his colleagues called their findings a vivid reminder that other "cryptic carnivores" may still await discovery.

Some animals once thought to be strictly herbivores are also revealing their carnivorous ways. Until recently, the tadpoles of most frog and toad species were assumed to be plant eaters, says associate biology professor Cy Mott, but new methodologies like fatty acid analyses and stable isotope analyses show otherwise. At Eastern Kentucky University, one of Mott's graduate students found that more than 70 percent of wood frog tadpoles' diets are composed of animal material. In studies of insect interactions on a native plant called ground cherry, State Arboretum of Virginia curator T'ai Roulston discovered that a caterpillar thought to be strictly fruit-eating deliberately eats a smaller caterpillar species inside the fruit. Not only that, but grasshoppers long believed to be exclusively herbivorous actively eat the

Tadpoles have specialized dental plates to scrape away algae from surfaces, but they also feed on fish, insects, and other tadpoles.

eggs of three-lined potato beetles on the leaves of the ground cherry. Is anyone really an herbivore anymore? "My list is getting smaller," Roulston says.

The act of eating itself can be risky. Given all the long-term dangers lurking in the tastescape, animals can get too much of a good thing. Though adding salt to a male butterfly's diet can increase his virility, one study found mixed effects of consuming roadside milkweeds, which take up excess salt from soil exposed to winter storm treatments: male caterpillars had more muscle growth and females

The driveway after a summer rain draws sleepy oranges, Eastern tiger swallowtails, cabbage whites, and many other butterflies.

had larger eyes, but overall survival rates were lower. More immediate hazards confront puddlers, as an intense focus on the task can make them vulnerable to predators. But there is power in the collective: puddling is a social behavior, and a study in Brazil showed reduced predation by birds as butterfly numbers increased.

The sociality of puddling is thought to be an attractant; if a butterfly sees his kind at a watering hole, he is more likely to touch down. But on that summer Sunday when my skin and sweat appeared to be making fine salt licks on every surface I touched, the diminutive blue butterflies who showed up were solo operators. How did they know where to go? The answer has been as elusive to scientists as it is to me. "We don't know anything about what attracts the first butterfly," Boggs says. Sodium has no scent, she notes, but maybe the butterflies are picking up associated scents like those of urea, ammonia, or bacteria. One of her students is exploring another possibility—that the lure could be visual. Salt affects the polarization of light, a characteristic that may be enough to draw the first pioneering butterfly.

Bittersweet: Plants Lure and Deter

"Come hither," says the late boneset, with its intoxicating, honeyish lure, a scent I've somehow failed to notice in the decade since it first showed up in our habitat. As sweet as a rose or lilac, but less cloying, it strikes me as the perfect floral perfume, and I suddenly understand its allure to insects.

Why I missed the boneset's scent until now is a mystery, but I can hazard a guess: flowers ingeniously emit volatiles at the time of day when their pollinators are most likely to be active, advertising their nectar supply in the hope that any takers will also transfer pollen from flower to flower on their abdomens, feet, proboscises, or other body parts that pick up and scatter about the tiny grains. For many years, that peak pollinating time fell during peak cubicle-sitting time for me.

Whatever the reason for my past nasal obliviousness, the same bonesets that delight the insects with heady aromas are usually repellent to deer. Though the compounds in the leaves benefit monarch butterflies, who extract them for defense against predators and parasitoids, mammals—including humans—would do well to avoid them. Chronic exposure through repeated ingestion of even small amounts of pyrrolizidine alkaloids can eventually lead to liver failure.

How could something so sweet also be so caustic? It's a clever survival strategy: make your flowers attractive to those tiny animals whose pollination services will help you reproduce, but embitter your leaves for the large ones who might chew you to nubs. The pyrrolizidine alkaloids in boneset are thought to impart an acrid taste, and for years that bitterness was all I smelled when handling or trimming the plants: not a bad scent but an earthy one, and certainly not something I'd be interested in putting in my mouth. Many other plants are selective in their guest lists, catering to those who have something to offer in return. Chile peppers produce capsaicin, which irritates mammals, whose digestive processing appears to destroy the seeds' ability to germinate. But the chemical compound doesn't bother birds, who are the seeds' primary dispersers.

Just as plants produce defenses to protect themselves against predators and pathogens, animals have strategies for avoiding, tolerating,

Generalist slugs aren't usually fans of milkweed, but it becomes more palatable after specialist insects, such as milkweed long-horned beetles and swamp milkweed leaf beetles, chew the leaves and deactivate the sticky, toxic latex.

or outwitting them. Generalists like deer eat a diversity of plants to get sufficient nutrients as well as to decrease the chance that they'll ingest too much of any particular toxin. Research on pollen chemistry has led scientists to conclude that the same might be true of generalist bees. Whereas specialist bees gather pollen from only one or a few related plant species, generalists like bumblebees hit up a wide variety of flowers, possibly to avoid accumulating too much of a specific compound. The flowers, in turn, might be ensuring that the bees don't become overeager and leave too little pollen for plant reproduction.

Plant response to herbivory is circumstantial, depending on what else is growing, who is eating, and when. Occasionally herbivores feast on plants they most often avoid; one fall when the usually toxic boneset first began spreading in our meadow, deer nibbled it to half its size. Given the time of year, that's probably not surprising, says Oswald Schmitz, a Yale University professor of population and community ecology. Plants defend themselves during peak season to maximize energy and preserve nutrient supplies to reproductive organs, a process that requires protecting photosynthetic tissue. Once mature and well-rooted, those that routinely die back for the winter don't need to persist aboveground for long in the fall. "So they actually reduce the production of the defense or actually resorb the defenses," says Schmitz, "and they become more palatable."

When they reappear in spring, many perennial plants don't tend to defend young shoots "until such time as there starts to be some nibbling," Schmitz notes. Investing in chemical defense means pulling energy away from growth and fitness functions, a trade-off a plant isn't likely to make until it becomes necessary. In the face of herbivory,

Leaving a few wilder paths and edges filled with tasty, vigorous plants helps feed rabbits while also directing them away from more vulnerable vegetation.

flower petals are often the first plant parts to be eaten, as they're the least-defended against browsing mammals. But even then, plants have a few tricks up their green sleeves for creative survival. They might increase production of chemical compounds, a resistance strategy, or they might take an approach known as tolerance, quickly making up for the loss by growing new plant tissue. They can even engage in phenological escape, timing their flowering, sprouting, or other important growth work for when herbivory is least likely to occur.

Browsing can trigger quick and prolific sprouting, as when sumacs or sassafras trees respond by sending up more suckers. Some perennials sprout multiple buds in the place of one nibbled flower—a fun process I witnessed after deer bit the tops off a few swamp sunflowers along a path in our meadow one September. A week later, four buds grew on each stem where there had been only one before, suggesting the plant might be engaging in a phenomenon known as "overcompensation." Such a response can reduce seed production in some situations and hamper the plant from growing as tall and reaching the sunlight. But it can also positively affect plants and their ability to spread, as illustrated by classic studies of the southwestern scarlet gilia (*Ipomopsis aggregata*). In the face of elk and mule deer foraging, this red bloomer produces significantly higher numbers of flowers and fruits, as well as greater root biomass, than uneaten plants produce. Herbivory by insects can have the same effect: in agricultural studies of potato cultivars, researchers have found that a certain amount of nibbling by Guatemalan tuber moth caterpillars can double the yield of potato farms.

Whether a plant can remain resilient depends on timing of browsing, extent of browsing, availability of other food sources to herbivores, size of plants, and soil conditions. Trade-offs between resistance and tolerance are common. A study by a University of Maryland assistant professor, Karin Burghardt, found that goldenrods grown in low nutrients no longer invested in chemical defense against grasshoppers, choosing instead to go underground. "They were investing in creating more individual rhizomes below ground to make individuals the next year.... They're just trying to run away as fast as they can to get back up to the levels of photosynthesis that will allow them to reproduce as much as they would have without the herbivore." The plants also produced thinner leaves, which are tastier to animals but more efficient at photosynthesizing. "So basically they're saying, 'I'm not going to defend myself; I'm in trouble if I get eaten again, but I will at least kind of get back some of my fitness I lost.'"

Just as animals can sense the mood and palatability of plants, plants can determine who's munching on them and adjust their defenses accordingly. Garden shears alone may not induce the same protective reaction as when a mammal takes a bite. Scientists have identified significant changes in plants' response to pruning when it's followed by exposure to animal saliva. Goat saliva caused the clipped shoots of red bushwillow trees in Botswana to grow three times as long as cut branches left untreated, and the plants grew more than twice as many leaves. Applying moose saliva to torn willow saplings in Sweden stimulated significantly more branching. In Germany, deer saliva increased the production of hormones in beech saplings and defense compounds in maple saplings.

Natural plant communities employ "associational defense" or "associational resistance" strategies to prevent insects and mammals from singling out any one species. Suckering plants like sumac and sassafras will even pop up among other plants as a way to gain a sort of strength in numbers. Schmitz has seen clonal species, like patches of goldenrods, send suckers far away into other patches to spread their genes and minimize the risk that they'll be wiped out in one dining session. Look at an old-field meadow, he notes, and you'll see a diversity of colorful wildflowers growing together rather than monoculture patches. "And you can even see this in high-deer-density areas," says Schmitz, noting that gardeners can mimic the same free-form growth. "It's about creating a neighborhood, a variety, so that any one herbivore won't necessarily look at all of the plants as really highly valuable or palatable. It's not like a rabbit going in a carrot field and saying, 'I'm just going to mow everything down.' You have to actually spend a lot of time finding that food item that is the most palatable to you."

Mixing tasty and untasty plants keeps
browsers guessing so that they don't eat too
much of any one species. In this meadow
garden, plants with strong chemical defenses,
such as blue mistflower and wild bergamot,
mingle with more palatable treats like
primroses and goldenrods.

Pokeweed is a perennial fan favorite,
beloved by wildlife but underappreciated
by humans. If you let it grow, it can
become a buffer plant, surrounding
vulnerable saplings.

Plants with lower chemical defenses can even physically borrow those of neighboring species. In the boreal forests of Finland and in controlled experiments, researchers found that "sticky" semivolatile compounds emitted from rhododendrons land on birch trees. Seedlings and leaves coated with these protective natural repellents hold on to their armor for hours and are less attractive to insect herbivores. This type of associational resistance could "help plants protect themselves as a result of coexistence," the authors noted. "This may support the idea that local plant/tree communities are coevolved with adaptation to the presence of their 'chemical neighbour.'"

Whether on land or in water, plants find strength in diversity. Even tasty seaweeds have been found to benefit from their proximity to less palatable cousins. A decades-old study on the North Carolina coast gleaned results that at first might seem counterintuitive: common plants had a protective effect on rarer ones. Seaweed species that grew abundantly but were unpalatable to fish created microsites, or a kind of refuge, for sought-after seaweeds that would be more vulnerable if left out by themselves in the open sea. By latching on to the more common species and growing as epiphytes—which use other plants for physical support but do not parasitize them—the rarer seaweeds may have made themselves more difficult for fish to locate.

Such findings point to the fallacy of the typical command-and-control style of landscaping and raise the question: Why do so many gardeners work at cross-purposes by removing vigorous plants that would provide refuge and protective barriers for some of the more vulnerable ones? Unpalatable species like bonesets or mountain mints can form protective shields around tastier sunflowers and penstemons when allowed to spread. And delicious plants like goldenrods or pokeweeds can create an edible buffer around irresistible oak saplings or young dogwoods, giving the deer something to eat while preserving other flowers for butterflies—and for you.

The Taste of Danger: Sex and Poison

If you head into our riotous habitat in mid-April—around April 16, to be exact—you might not be aware of the extraordinary events unfolding at your feet. You'll surely sense some of the other wonders of springtime: the first columbines opening, preparing for the hummingbirds' imminent arrival. The mild scent of the woodland phlox calling out to hummingbird moths. The squeaking of the male toads who've accidentally tried to mate with each other, underscored by the scratchy-throated insistence of nuthatches and tufted titmice trying to reclaim territory from bluebirds establishing a new nest site.

But to see a truly epic springtime ritual, you'll have to look down and look closely. There on the ground, you'll find all the elements of a great spy thriller—a tale of sex and seduction, thievery and weaponry, false identity and fatal deception—wrapped into two small miracles of nature known to scientists as *Meloe campanicollis* and *Pedilus terminalis*, plus some unwitting bee victims. To the rest of us, or at least to those of us who are curious enough to look them up, they're known as a blister beetle and a fire-colored beetle.

The day Will first spots them under our ailing ash tree in 2017, they're attached at the hip, or rather, at the abdomen and the elytra, the term for beetles' hardened forewings. Wherever a blister beetle

Fire-colored beetles hop atop a blister beetle, presumably to lap up the cantharidin that oozes from his body. Toxic to people, the substance is important in courtship and defense activities of some insects.

exudes orange droplets of a substance called cantharidin, the tiny fire-colored beetles want a taste of the action, hopping along for the ride as the blister beetles scurry among the buttercups and fleabanes. Though it looks like fun to my human eyes, this is serious business. If the fire-colored beetles play their cards right, that sexy cantharidin they're stealing off the backs of the blister beetles might even help them find a mate. Once thought to be an aphrodisiac and marketed as "Spanish fly," cantharidin can sicken and kill humans but is a potent defense for the only known producers of it—beetles in the Meloidae and Oedemeridae (or false blister beetle) families—as well as for "canthariphilous" insects, some of whom also use the substance in courtship.

The first time I see this unfamiliar drama unfolding, I fall back on known frames of reference to try to understand its meaning. Rather than a steamy tale of love and war, the bulky blister beetles toting their tiny hangers-on remind me of the sweet maternal instincts of other creatures: mother opossums who carry their kids on their backs while foraging, and wolf spiders whose hatchlings cling to them for weeks until they're ready to venture out on their own.

But these insect hitchhikers are no mini-mes; they look nothing like the black blister beetles. They're much smaller and sport bright red thoraxes, true to both the common name and the scientific name of their family, Pyrochroidae. Unlike blister beetles, who biosynthesize cantharidin entirely on their own, fire-colored beetles don't have that ability, and so they steal it. Cantharidin can help them deter predators such as other insects and birds, and it may also be given as a nuptial offering to be passed along to eggs, a behavior that's been documented in related species.

Though the interaction might be widespread, occurring in places throughout the world, hardly anyone ever sees it. "All through history, there are very few observations," says Leslie Saul-Gershenz, an ecologist who documented the same behavior between two similar species, *Meloe franciscanus* and *Pedilus punctulatus*, in California. "Not to say that it's not happening all the time; it's just that humans aren't observing it." When her paper on the subject was published in 2004, only fourteen such sightings had been made since 1827.

Yet two years after our first observation, this time while I am kneeling to admire the sublime emergence of spring wildflowers in the patio beds, I see the fire-colored beetles riding piggyback on the blister beetles again. It's the same time of year, almost to the day: April 17. The blister beetle's elytra look a bit chewed on the edges, no doubt the work of a whole crew of fire-colored beetles leeching off him. The next day, I'll see more blister beetles in the same spot, running through the decaying leaves to destinations only they know. The uncanny timing is no coincidence. "I could set my watch to the date that they emerge," says Saul-Gershenz of the *Meloe* species she has studied. "They're like clockwork."

To get what they need, fire-colored beetles have to make an appearance and be ready to mate during the narrow time frame when the blister beetles are out and about. The window of opportunity is even slimmer than that, though, because blister beetles also have their own deadlines to meet. They must emerge when native bees are out mating and provisioning their nests; without bee nests to parasitize, the blister beetles can't reproduce. "It's a very finely tuned system," says Saul-Gershenz. It's so finely tuned, in fact, that after spending a total of three months observing beetle and bee interactions in the Mojave Desert, Saul-Gershenz worked for five years to untangle the chemistry behind it.

What she discovered was astounding, going far beyond the standard narrative about the life cycle of beetles in the Meloidae family. That story follows a simpler trajectory that some entomology resources still repeat: a blister beetle triungulin—the term for a first-stage larva—emerges from an egg buried underground and crawls up a plant stem and onto a flower. There, he waits for a bee to land on the flower. Then he hops onto that bee and, presuming it's a female, ends up in a bee nest, where he eats the pollen and nectar stores and sometimes the bee larvae too.

That may be true enough for some blister beetle species, but Saul-Gershenz found something even more intricate while studying *M. franciscanus*. In that species, the triungulins emerge, crawl up a plant stem, aggregate into a shape that approximates the shape of the host bee species they're trying to attract, and collectively release a scent similar to the pheromones of the female bee of that species. When a male bee responds, tricked into thinking he's seeing and smelling a potential mate, the beetle babies latch on. Unlucky in love, the male bee tries again, this time with an actual bee, and the triungulins hop onto the hapless female, who carries them to her nest. "How that all evolved is just really incredible," says Saul-Gershenz. "It's just an amazing example of the coevolution of parasite and host."

Since Saul-Gershenz's discovery, scientists in Europe have documented triungulins of at least two more blister beetle species aggregating on plant stems in a similar manner: one species in France appeared to be mimicking bees, and another in Germany appeared to be mimicking the shapes and colors of flowers. Depending on their location, blister beetles parasitize different types of bees; some go after plasterer bees, and others infiltrate mining or digger bee nests. Saul-Gershenz has found that *M. franciscanus* beetles can even adjust their perching heights on stems to the flying altitudes of their host bee species, increasing their chances of successful trickery.

Whether the blister beetle triungulins in my backyard are luring bees through collective deception or simply waiting passively for them to land on a flower remains to be seen, since little is known about most of the *Meloe* species, their interactions with other organisms, and canthariphilous insects in general. We don't even know exactly how our resident fire-colored beetles are courting and mating once they've stolen the goods from the blister beetles. The most we can do for now is speculate, based on the documented activities of related species.

The female of the *Neopyrochroa flabellata* species, another fire-colored beetle, wastes no time in sizing up whether a male is all flash and no substance. Her quick test involves grabbing onto him, sinking her teeth into the cleft between his eyes, where cantharidin is stored, and eating the contents. If the toxin is present, she's ready to mate. If not, she refuses the dejected suitor. Females of the species *Notoxus monoceros*, members of a related family known as the Anthicids, are equally decisive in their demands, biting the elytra glands of the males to assess their cantharidin loads before agreeing to a hot romance.

Even the original source of the cantharidin is still an open question, though it's clear that blister beetles are an important supplier to many species. "But the possibility cannot be ruled out that cantharidin is available to cantharidiphiles from entirely different, as yet unknown sources," wrote the late chemical ecologist Thomas Eisner and his coauthors in *Secret Weapons: Defenses of Insects, Spiders, Scorpions, and Other Many-Legged Creatures*. Those sources may be surprising: though cantharidin is thought to protect insects from pathogenic fungi, other types of fungi might actually be supplementing their defenses with more cantharidin.

Who can say for sure? Only the beetles themselves, and that's why we have to study them—very carefully. Though generally harmless to humans, their secretions can pack a painful punch if touched. Art Evans, author of *Beetles of Eastern North America*, once assumed his tough fingers could handle the cantharidin but then made the mistake of wiping his brow and blistering his eyelids. Even when he's tried to be more careful in the field, he recalls being jolted awake by the sensation that "somebody had taken a lit match or a cigarette right across the base of my neck."

As biological weapons go, these mechanisms are fairly benign, at least for us. The beetles are just defending themselves, trying to survive in a beetle-eat-beetle-eat-bee world. Still, for now, I'm content to admire them from a distance, searching for their nests and trying to figure out who their bee hosts might be, grateful that the beetles have let me in on at least a few of their secrets.

Eat and Be Eaten: How Feeding Enhances Diversity

It's been seventeen years since the cicadas have seen the light, when they descended from the trees to tunnel into the soil around the roots. It's been seventeen days since I last told my father I loved him, the grand finale in a season of departures that started with the deaths of my aunt and then an old friend from cancer. I'm ready for a sign, a reminder from nature that life is still here, vibrant and resilient. Tonight seems like as good a time as any for a ghostly reemergence.

Coming up the front path after work, Will calls my name excitedly through the screen door. As I step out to meet him, I have to be careful where I walk. The ground has come alive with an entire cicada nation, and several cicadas begin crawling up my boots as they look for a place to hang their hats (and eventually their shells). Wandering slowly around our silver maple, we see that some have already been

This ghostlike cicada has just emerged from her old exoskeleton after spending seventeen years underground.

Cicada shells, which eventually add nutrients back to the soil, collect under a Virginia creeper vine in the crotch of a silver maple.

aboveground for a few days and are now undergoing their final molt, pushing their way out of their lobster-like exoskeletons and looking like pale zombies.

If he could, Will would start jumping out of his own skin too. That's how riveted he is by the mass arrival of *Magicicada septendecim*. But not everyone is caught up in their spell. "So cool! Come look!" he's still exclaiming when a friend shows up at the end of the driveway and signals her disapproval.

"Are you looking at cicadas? They are terrible! We're killing them!" she calls out. Her words are painful, and I try to ignore them, but she keeps going. "They killed two of our trees seventeen years ago! We don't want them to kill more trees!" Forced away from my therapeutic reverie, I mention all the good that cicadas do: they don't really kill trees, they just give them a haircut. They aerate the soil with all their burrowing. They feed other animals and plants, which eventually receive a boost from the nitrogen-containing exoskeletons of newly hatched cicadas and the bodies of dead cicadas, who—a few weeks from now—will decompose back into the same earth they crawled out of. And though I don't know it yet, I'll come to learn this summer just how blissful their symphony is, how grateful I am to hear the mating calls of cicadas drown out the neighborhood mowers, and how much fun it is to watch a cicada full of watery tree sap walk across the back of your chair, pause deliberately, and take a squat before continuing on his journey.

All the arguments in the world aren't likely to be heard by someone whose mind is already made up, so each morning for the next couple of weeks we see our friend and her husband walking around beating their few trees with broomsticks, hoping to vanquish the insects in buckets. They say cicadas are in endless supply, but they haven't heard the reports from Long Island yet, where these ancient insects have been all but eliminated, likely by development and habitat destruction.

To human eyes, voracious feeding may seem alarming, but taking the long view fosters appreciation for the intricate relationships that unfold in a world of insatiable appetites. Many of the links in the food chain are indirect, requiring years of study to untangle. It might be surprising to learn that deer mice are important propagators of blueberries in Alaska after they pick up the seeds in bear scat, but it's straightforward enough. What's less intuitive is that those fruits also may owe their abundance to salmon, who draw the bears to the coastal riparian areas where the blueberries grow.

Bears can help plants in other ways, including by eating ants. The relationship is anything but linear and required the creative work of ecologist Joshua Grinath, now an assistant professor at Idaho State University, to piece together. In western US habitats, tiny insects known as treehoppers suck sugary sap from the plant tissue of shrubs known as rabbitbrushes, excreting the excess. This delicious honey-dew is a delicacy for ants, and they show their gratitude for the treat by acting as bodyguards and preying on crab spiders, lady beetles, and other arthropods who would otherwise eat the treehoppers. But the ants themselves are tasty to another predator: bears. In experiments in Colorado, Grinath found that when bears disturb ant nests, diminishing the number of ant bodyguards, the arthropod predators move in to eat the defenseless treehoppers. Freed from the hungry mouths of so many treehoppers, the rabbitbrush grows, potentially nourishing and sheltering even more wildlife: bees, butterflies, birds, deer, antelope, elk, deer, sage grouse, and jackrabbits.

Human encroachment—in the form of urban sprawl, hunting, and accidental food handouts from bird feeders and unsealed garbage—already poses a challenge to bears and exacerbates conflicts with people. Could our unnecessarily disruptive relationship with bears also affect plant life? Grinath and his team think so. "In recent decades, bears in Colorado have increased their consumption of human-derived foods while decreasing their consumption of insects," they wrote. "We expect that in locations where bears rely heavily on food from humans or decrease in abundance, the strength of cascades on plants may weaken, potentially shifting plant diversity."

Even the presence of fish in ponds can affect the growth of nearby plants, leading to increased pollination. Dragonflies have big appetites for insects, including pollinators, but fish have big appetites for dragonfly larvae. By reducing dragonfly populations, fish inadvertently protect more insects from predation, freeing them up to visit flowers, according to a study conducted in a Florida reserve. If fewer dragonflies mean more pollinators in the immediate area, you might think that's a reason to add fish to your pond. But no story in nature is as simple as that. Fewer dragonflies might mean more mosquitoes, as dragonflies are a major mosquito predator. And adding fish also makes ponds inhospitable to frogs, who are gobbled up at the tadpole stage. What's more, the researchers noted, the plant community around a pond doesn't necessarily benefit from more pollination: "By increasing the reproductive success of insect-pollinated plants, freshwater fish introductions potentially alter competitive relationships between terrestrial plants, putting plants not pollinated by insects at a competitive disadvantage. Wetland destruction can harm dragonfly populations, with similar consequences for terrestrial plants."

Though usually well intentioned, human attempts to protect single species from being eaten often disregard the balance created by dynamic communities. When aphids snack on common milkweed, the plants' defenses are substantially reduced, benefiting monarch caterpillar growth. Conversely, caterpillar feeding can have the opposite effect, inducing defenses that inhibit aphid growth. Those findings are likely to surprise gardeners convinced that aphids are harming the monarch food supply, but science continues to show the importance of diversity. In another study, an abundant community of aphids, leafhoppers, and other plant-eating arthropods on milkweed was found to increase the survival of monarchs hatched on the same plants, likely because of something known as the dilution effect: when predators have a plethora of prey available, monarch caterpillars are not always their first choice.

Among the least appreciated diners are parasites, but their feeding habits can enhance critical ecosystem functions. Horned passalus beetles, found in logs throughout the eastern United States and parts of Canada, break down wood better when nematodes live inside their bodies. Also called patent leather beetles because of their gorgeous shine, they have a family-oriented lifestyle that's rare in the insect world. Both parents help raise their young in a log, on a diet of chewed-up decaying wood and frass. They ensure that the children's pupal chambers—their bedrooms during the last stage of life before adulthood—are well located and protected. Sometimes young adults stay with their parents for several months, a long time in the life of an animal who lives an average of one year. They even communicate through a dozen or more different sounds, described by some as squeaky and "kissy" noises, to convey disturbance, aggression, and courtship.

Bess beetles eat decaying wood. They live in family groups, a rarity in the insect world.

An ebony jewelwing damselfly looks out for lunch. The eating habits of predatory insects can affect what kinds of plants grow around a pond.

A naturally occurring parasitic nematode known as *Chondronema passali* makes its home in 70 to 90 percent of these important decomposers, yet the beetles are mostly unaffected. "They've got a lot of parasites, but this one is really crazy, and it is so abundant within each beetle. A single beetle can have thousands of these little worms wiggling around inside it, and it's a perfectly normal beetle," says the University of Georgia's Andy Davis. "For many years I've been trying to figure out: How can these beetles get by when they're so heavily parasitized?"

Davis has found that in times of acute stress, parasitized beetles aren't as good at escaping predators or fighting off rival males. But they're otherwise resilient, and he and a student discovered why: the insects make up for the loss of energy by scarfing down more food. In experiments comparing unparasitized with parasitized beetles, the researchers found that each day, the parasitized beetles processed 15 percent more wood into sawdust. They were also a bit larger. By returning nutrients to the earth faster, they're fulfilling their roles more effectively, Davis concluded. "If you think about it from the ecosystem's perspective, it's kind of a good thing because the beetle's job, so to speak, is to chew up old logs and to turn them into soil," he says. "And so beetles that have these wormies basically do a better job."

As the husband of a University of Georgia scientist who studies parasites, Davis has developed something of an affection for them. "At some point you just start to like parasites if you're married to my wife," he says. The number of parasites in the world far outweighs nonparasites, yet in science classrooms across the country, there is usually no mention of them during discussions of food webs, he laments. "There's so many of them, but yet we don't really appreciate them;

we don't really appreciate what they do. And they're probably just as important in an ecosystem as the average predator is because they also keep populations of animals in check by reducing their health or simply killing them, just as much as a predator does."

The plant kingdom also has its share of beneficial moochers. Hemiparasitic plants photosynthesize on their own and don't appear to be any different from other species when seen aboveground. But by infiltrating the roots of their hosts, they acquire water and nutrients, increasing the plants' competitive race to the top to see the light. In native and restored grasslands, the presence of hemiparasites can increase floristic diversity by reducing the biomass of dominant wildflowers or grasses and opening up space for other species. Researchers have explored their potential as "pseudograzers," or species that can change the structures of plant communities the way buffaloes and other plant eaters do.

Because horned passalus beetles spend their lives mostly in the dark, leaving logs only to find a mate or a new home, it's not easy to cross paths with them. But in midsummer, as the cicadas are winding down for the season, their symphonies reduced to solos, Will asks me to identify a shiny black beetle heading down the newly wood-chipped walkway to the memorial garden we dedicated to my father. She's a horned passalus beetle, or as I like to call her, a bess beetle— another name for this species that's thought to derive from the French and old English words for "kiss," a reference to the sounds they make. I wonder if she has just left her family. Does she miss them? Will she find a suitable new log home in our habitat? I ponder her future as I walk back to the patio to write. A dying cicada falls on my leg, and I sit with her for the next hour as life slowly leaves her, knowing that soon the ants will carry her away. She'll become a part of the soil too, joining cicada nymphs who are already attaching themselves to the tree roots underground, safe for the next seventeen years from the long arm of human capriciousness and broomsticks.

Supply and Demand

It's a rare being who intentionally wants to smell like poo and rotting flesh, but that's the goal of the orange creatures pushing up out of the soil and into the expansive autumn light. Fruiting bodies of stinkhorn fungi, they're as bright as the stripes on my seventh-grade gym shorts but much more beautiful, their colors crossing a sunset gradient of orange-yellow crayon to near-pink. In form and structure, they look every bit as much like male appendages as their scientific name, *Phallus rugulosus*, implies. Capped by a brown, gooey spore mass known as a gleba, the mushrooms clearly have an agenda, and as I kneel down to look through my camera, I see that the goo is covered in flies.

Stinkhorns are helpful organisms to have in the garden, nourishing not just flies but also plants. Like the horned passalus beetles, they eat organic matter. But rather than ingesting it, they absorb it by sending out threadlike filaments called hyphae and secreting digestive enzymes. In the process, they convert decaying plants into nutrients. Aboveground, the stinkhorns recruit flies to help them reproduce. By producing compounds with scents that mimic the stuff of fly fine dining, the fungi lay the groundwork for the spreading of spores through fly feet and excrement.

The gooey spore mass of a stinkhorn fungus
attracts flies, who aid in the spread of fungi,
which in turn enhance the soil.

Flies also offer many talents, among them their abilities to clean up carrion and scat, prey upon other insects, and pollinate plants—a vastly underappreciated service that they can sometimes perform even better than bees. Despite those benefits, some gardeners find stink-horn fungi and the insects who enjoy them highly offensive. But we couldn't smell the mushrooms at all, and their hangers-on were as disinterested in me as I was fascinated by them, so I whiled away an afternoon keeping an up-close eye on the flies.

As they sponged up the thick liquid through their soft mouth parts, they seemed quite content to share the feast. Some left while others arrived, and whenever the numbers teetered off-balance and the flies got a little too close to one another for comfort, they had a polite way to claim their territory. Houseflies have chemoreceptors to assess food palatability through their feet, compound eyes to detect light and motion, and hairs all over their body to sense air flow and judge distance from objects. Never taking their mouthparts or their eyes off the mushroom prize, the flies who felt too boxed in would lift a leg and then slowly, gracefully bring it back down, a kind of gentle seesawing to keep from being stepped on. Occasionally another fly advanced anyway, resulting in a tussle of the limbs, but neither fly diverged from the engrossing task of devouring the goo. Studies on fruit flies call this "fencing" and describe it as an aggressive behavior, but to me these larger houseflies just seemed mildly irritated, their gesture akin to a human absentmindedly swatting at the air.

Elsewhere in the garden, personal space is at more of a premium, as when two large monarch caterpillars munch the last of the leaves atop a swamp milkweed one late summer afternoon. Straddling the same stem, they come face-to-face for a brief moment, and one begins lunging at the other one, similar to the way our dog used to deliver warning nips to her sworn feline enemy when he sauntered past her food bowl. Neuroscientist Alex Keene published a paper exploring the cause of such aggression after seeing it in his garden and discovering that food scarcity is the trigger. What implications that might have for whole populations in an age of dwindling plants is unknown, but in our garden it's easy enough to move the caterpillars a few feet away, where an abundance of leaves allows them to resume their nibbling without violent incident.

On a broader scale, animals and plants devise ingenious ways to regulate supply and demand. The mass emergence of periodical cicadas is timed to ensure survival of the species; so many congregate in the trees at once that there's no way their natural predators can eat them all. Some animals certainly seem to try, though, making a boom year of easy eats for squirrels and birds and others who don't have to travel more than a foot or two to find a slow-moving meal.

Plants appear to have a similar strategy, though the timing of their bounties is more sporadic and difficult for us humans to gauge. During what are known as mast years, when oaks, hickories, walnuts, or beeches produce huge quantities of nuts simultaneously, food supply exceeds demand from squirrels, jays, chipmunks, deer, and other nut predators—likely a deliberate tactic for ensuring enough nuts remain to start a new generation of trees. Maples follow a similar pattern, blanketing the understory with the yellow clusters of their progeny, and in some years our squirrels can't keep up, twirling them around like pinwheels in front of their faces to get the most of the all-you-can-eat buffet. Animal populations grow in turn, and those higher up the food chain—foxes, hawks, coyotes—also are fortified

In a mast year, squirrels can't keep up with all the maple seeds.

by the bounty of abundant prey. But masting occurs anywhere from every two to seven years, give or take a few, and during the times in between, sometimes no nuts are produced at all, leaving nut lovers with little to eat and once again bringing animal populations back down to size.

If masting trees are nature's risk strategists, then flowers might be the skilled regulators. A flower's chemical composition and coloration aren't the only traits influencing which creatures are invited to eat and which ones are shown the exit door before they ever reach the dinner table. More than twenty thousand plant species around the world restrict access to their flowers by hiding pollen within their anthers. Only those bees with the capability of whipping up a tornado of vibrations—a behavior known as buzz pollination or sonication—can open up the small slits at the tips of the anthers to get to the goodness inside.

Many flowers invest in nectar to lure insects, who then inadvertently transfer pollen grains to stigmas while foraging. In this mutual exchange, the sweet reward helps ensure fertilization so the plants can set seed and reproduce. But it also invites everybody in town to the party, sometimes at too much cost to the host. "If you're providing nectar, anybody can eat nectar," says Roulston, whose research includes bee ecology. "So you've got this investment in reward, and you may get ants taking it and small flies and small bees that are too small to actually contact the reproductive parts." Though all of those insects are capable of pollinating certain plants, they aren't a good fit for every flower, and they may not be as efficient as some of their larger counterparts.

Most buzz-pollinated plants avoid the hassle of hosting loafers by being nectarless. But producing pollen is costly too, requiring substantial energy, so they make the bees work for it. Because of their size and fuzziness, bumblebees are exceptionally well suited to the task, but carpenter bees, sweat bees, and mining bees also buzz pollinate. By vibrating their flight muscles at a high frequency, they coax out a torrent of pollen grains—enough to bring back to their nests as well as to scatter about on other blooms they subsequently visit.

Clearly this up-close-and-personal interaction is good for the plants, but why would the bees expend so much effort when other flowers freely offer the pollen and nectar they need for themselves and their larval provisions? One explanation may be the quality of the pollen. Scientists at Penn State's Center for Pollinator Research have found that bumblebees intentionally seek pollen with a high protein-to-lipid ratio. Proteins and lipids are critical to bees' reproduction and development, and the bees adjust their foraging decisions

Wild senna doesn't release its treats to just anybody, saving its pollen for native bees who can buzz pollinate the flowers.

The high-pitched sounds of happy bees emanate from our front-yard senna patch in midsummer.

accordingly, switching up their flower choices to try to meet their nutritional needs. In field observations and lab experiments, the bees' greatest preferences were for wild senna (*Senna hebecarpa*) and spiderwort (*Tradescantia ohiensis*), both buzz-pollinated plants. The blooms of these plants don't produce nectar, wrote the researchers, "suggesting that they may have evolved to produce high quality pollen as their only reward for pollination."

And what a pleasing reward it must be, judging by the frenzied rush around the wild sennas in our garden each July. It's a mad-dash pub crawl of sonicators catching a buzz, as entire plants practically shake with the high-pitched drilling sounds of bumblebees and sweat bees bursting open the pollen stores. Noticeably absent from the crowd are honeybees, who are unable to buzz pollinate and thus stay away entirely—a good thing, since the increasing presence of these domesticated insects in residential communities threatens the wild bees who remain.

In the flower-deprived landscapes of the suburbs, casual beekeepers are contributing to an inventory crisis. Most of the four thousand native bee species in North America are solitary nesters, laying their eggs in inconspicuous spots in the ground, plant stalks and twigs, or cavities in dead wood. By contrast, a typical honeybee colony is made up of twenty thousand to eighty thousand individuals, and those bees gather an amount of pollen that would feed a hundred thousand progeny of an average solitary bee species—a drastic drain on limited floral resources. Studies have shown that honeybees often displace foraging native bees, who may visit fewer flowers than they normally would, gather less pollen, and experience lower reproductive success. One California researcher found strong evidence linking higher numbers of honeybees with the local decline of two bumble-bee populations.

Originally introduced from Europe for wax and honey production, honeybees are the subject of intense cultural and financial focus, perpetuated by the beekeeping industry and the greenwashing campaigns of pesticide companies. "Save the Bee" initiatives have confused the public into thinking they have to suit up in body armor and buy smokers to help pollinators, when the solution is a lot simpler: stop mowing everything down, let the flowers grow again, and nurture the bees who already live in your community.

Though honeybees have been credited for the lion's share of pollination on farms, native bees are often more efficient pollinators. A recent study of seven major US crops showed that, in most cases, the contribution of wild native bees is similar to or even higher than that of honeybees—perhaps not surprising, since we've long known that native bees are important for food staples like tomatoes, blueberries, and squash. Native plant communities may also be affected when honeybees dominate; one study of California coastal sage scrub found that honeybee foraging behaviors can disrupt plant-pollination networks and lead to low seed set. Their pollination activities may also exacerbate the spread of invasive plants that encroach on wildlife habitat.

It's not the honeybees' fault—far from it. They didn't ask to live in boxes and be transported all over the country like chattel, subjected to the kinds of pathogens and parasites that intense captivity can foster. They don't have a choice, but the rest of us do. Honeybees may still be an integral part of our agricultural systems, but they don't have to be an integral part of our home landscapes.

Dispersal and Disruption

By September our deck becomes a carnival. In the mornings it's not uncommon to see the world's tiniest pole vaulter, Mr. Chippie, making running leaps to nab the juicy red berries hanging from the lowest parts of the coral honeysuckle vine. In the afternoons, as temperatures rise, an Eastern comma butterfly hangs upside down and sinks her proboscis into one of the vine's overripe fruits. A bumblebee engages in "nectar robbing," drinking from a hole made at the base of a red flower without pollinating in return. Someone bounces in and out of the leaves before settling into the honeysuckle's dense foliage—a tiny tree frog taking a break from the crowd.

Lording over all of it from atop the deck rail, unseen by anyone but me, is a bee-mimicking robber fly. His camouflage protects him from beephobic predators while also obscuring his impending nefarious activities, which generally involve capturing another insect, injecting him with neurotoxins and enzymes that immobilize and liquefy him, and sucking down the remains like a smoothie.

For all the bounty, this ragtag bunch have ruby-throated hummingbirds, the vine's super pollinators, to thank. Every few minutes, the stars of the show swoop in, and when they're not sparring for territory, they make their way from one flower to the next abruptly and efficiently.

The coevolution of hummingbirds and their plant partners is unmistakable. About seven thousand plant species from Alaska to Patagonia rely on the birds to transfer pollen as they forage from flower to flower for nectar. Long hummingbird beaks and the tubular blooms of their favorite species in my habitat—coral honeysuckle,

Bee-mimicking robber flies pretend they're part of the gentle herbivorous crowd so they can sneak up on unsuspecting prey.

cardinal flowers, columbine, bee balm—are obviously made for each other, so much so that if I happen to be adjusting a vine when a hummingbird wants to eat, I'm nearly dive-bombed for my rudeness.

It's possible to view such antics up close without ever hanging a feeder, especially in a yard filled with native plants. It may be preferable too. Artificial feeding can have untold impacts on animals and plants alike. Disease transmission is the one that's become most painfully obvious, as an increasing number of outbreaks are reported among different species across North America. Unnaturally high numbers of birds at seed and nectar feeders can turn them into breeding grounds for pathogens, spreading salmonellosis, trichomoniasis, avian pox, and other diseases. Feeders can also cause unnecessary and tragic conflicts, inspiring battles between humans and any mammal or nonnative bird who dares to swing by for a snack.

Natural foods are likely more nutritious as well. When California scientists compared plant nectar with the sugar water mixtures used in feeders, they found different microbial communities, indicating that artificial feeding may alter gut microbiomes, with unknown consequences for the gastrointestinal health of hummingbirds. Too much focus on feeders at the expense of native plants presents another problem for birds: native plants draw a whole community of insects and spiders that most birds, including hummingbirds, need for protein and for raising their young.

Without their hummingbird partners, plants themselves can suffer. In a study in a suburban park near Mexico City, scientists observed the impact of feeders on two native species of salvias, a genus of plants that also have long, tubular flowers. In the presence of feeders, hummingbird visitation to the blooms of both species decreased, and one species produced fewer seeds. (The other was visited by bees as well, who likely compensated for the hummingbirds' absence.)

Ecologists in Costa Rica have also found that free fast food draws hummingbirds away from their normal flower-visiting activities, a shift that could dramatically affect the plants' ability to reproduce. One study showed that in the presence of feeders, the birds carried little to no pollen, and when they did, it was mostly from one species. Many of the birds appeared to be traveling a considerable distance to the feeders, bypassing flowers along the way.

"The competitive and antagonistic pattern observed between feeders and flowers shows that natural pollination systems are being significantly altered by the use of feeders," wrote Gerardo Avalos, center director of the School for Field Studies in Costa Rica, in a summary of the research. "Supplementing hummingbirds with food seems likely to interfere with pollination networks already stressed by many anthropogenic effects, including global warming." Using feeders carefully and temporarily can be educational, he added, "but please don't make them addicts to cheap food. Plant a hummingbird garden, or even better, go out bird watching."

It seems reasonable to assume that feeders for other birds might have similar downstream effects, changing the dynamics of seed dispersal and habitat restoration. Birds in gardens and natural habitats spread seed by knocking it about while snacking on seedheads, processing it in their intestines and scattering it in their droppings, and transferring it to distant locations on their feathers and feet. By encouraging birds to spend too much of their precious time eating the same few types of seeds in one place—and often nonnative seeds, at that—feeders could be hampering the spread of the very plants that those birds rely on for survival.

Plant dispersers come in many forms that we frequently fail to appreciate. Among the litany of transgressions blamed on deer is the notion that they spread invasive plants. It's not a very balanced conclusion, given the architects of that phenomenon: humans, whose global movement and aesthetic desires are solely responsible for spreading plants all over the world at a rapid clip. Lost in the half-truths about the animals and plants that many people love to hate are the positive flip sides: in this case, the fact that deer and other species plant natives too. When animals travel through our habitat, we find native wildflowers and berrying shrubs and trees sprouting in their footsteps: Geums, Saniculas, enchanter's nightshade, false nettle, blue mistflower, blue-eyed grass, path rush, clasping Venus's looking glass, jumpseed, violets, Lobelias, goldenrods, Eastern woodland sedge, yellow fumewort, fleabanes, frost asters, cinnamon willowherb, blackberries, raspberries, pokeweed, black cherries, pin oaks, Eastern red cedars, tulip trees, walnuts, hickories, and many others each year.

In conventionally managed, mowed spaces, these plants don't stand much of a chance—just one of the many problems they now face in their struggle to keep up with a changing Earth. Centuries of colonization, industrialization, and land and animal abuse have obscured the value of forgotten native flora and, along with them, the value of their greatest animal partners. More than half of all plant species are dispersed by animals, but habitat loss, logging, hunting, and human introduction of plant species outside their natural range have led to local and global extinctions, a process that scientists have reduced to a devastating four-syllable word: *defaunation*. Climate change greatly exacerbates the loss. Future survival will likely rely on plants' ability to migrate to places with temperature and moisture conditions that can still meet their needs, and their seeds will have to travel farther in animal poop and on wings, feet, and feathers to keep up. But researchers have found that the decline of animal populations has already reduced plants' ability to make those journeys by 60 percent, and if currently threatened and endangered seed-dispersing birds and mammals go extinct, that reduction would drop by another 15 percent.

The effects of climate change and habitat loss go far beyond our normal field of vision and well into the forest floor, where some of the tiniest allies of plants are busy spreading the seeds of violets, bloodroots, trilliums, spring beauties, wild gingers, and other spring wildflowers in the understory. In going about their daily routines, ants disperse the seeds of an estimated eleven thousand species worldwide. This activity has a fancy name—myrmecochory—and a fan club of fascinated scientists working to unravel its mysteries.

Relationships between plants and the ants who move their seeds around are often mutualistic. In return for the ants' efforts, the plants

Elderberry spreads with the help of mockingbirds and other animals, who disperse the seeds in their droppings.

reward them with fleshy, lipid- and protein-filled appendages on their seeds called elaiosomes, which the ants feed to their larvae before carrying the seeds away from the nest. In the process, the seeds are deposited in new, often nutrient-rich places. They're released from the shade of parent and sibling plants so they don't have to compete for light. They're protected from rodents and slugs who might eat them without dispersing them further. They mingle with unrelated individuals, increasing the genetic diversity of their species. And they can even get some good medicine; recent research has found that the antiseptic qualities of chemicals secreted from ants' glands can kill pathogens.

It's not all peace, love, and harmony in the ant-plant relationship, though. Cheaters and opportunists appear to abound on both sides. To lure ants, plants with juicy elaiosomes emit chemical cues, including oleic acid, the same substance that triggers ants to carry corpses out of their nests. Some plants with reduced or no elaiosomes use these signals too, enticing ants into service and offering little if any reward in return. Deceit is a two-way street, though, and certain ants—including the yellow-footed ant, a species accidentally introduced from Asia and first found in Philadelphia more than eighty years ago—have been found to eat elaiosomes without dispersing attached seeds.

Human activity appears to be dramatically altering the scene of these internecine dramas. In eastern deciduous forests, 30 to 40 percent of herbaceous understory plants are propagated through myrmecochory. Ants of the *Aphaeonogaster* genus are considered keystone dispersers in this ecosystem, distributing up to 70 percent of the seeds of those plants. But on lands cleared in the past for agricultural use, studies are showing that the ant populations aren't what they used to be. In Ohio, forests that have been regenerating for eighty years still harbor lower concentrations of seed-dispersing ants than mature hardwood forests. These newer forests also have higher concentrations of introduced earthworms, who eat fallen leaves more quickly than native worms, removing from the forest floor the cover and refuge that ants need. In studies in New York and New Jersey, the story is similar: *Aphaeonogaster* ants are more abundant and seed dispersal rates are significantly higher in primary forests—those that have never been cleared—than in secondary ones. But a reduced presence of ants isn't the only problem: in experiments at the forest edges, increased numbers of introduced slugs, who render seeds unattractive to ants by eating the elaiosomes, seem to also depress seed dispersal rates.

Habitat differences play a significant role. Secondary forests contain fewer leaves and logs for ants to colonize than forests that have remained intact, says Carmela Buono, a doctoral candidate in ecology at Binghamton University. "If I had to poll ant colonies, at least for the keystone dispersers, logs are the ideal habitat because they're nice and moist, and they're soft and easy to nest in," says Buono, who has been leading some of the studies. "So I could really see [the absence of] all of that at least making it more difficult for the ants to reinhabit a forest patch."

Even in the altered suburban landscape, it's not hard to observe the positive effects of leaving stumps, lining paths with logs, and creating brush piles. When neighbors cut trees, we place pieces of the trunk around our garden, making lemons from lemonade and even attracting ants who emit a lemony scent from glands near their mandibles when disturbed. The compound, called citronellal, acts as an alarm call to ants, who rush to defend the colony. Known as citronella ants, yellow ants, or lemon ants, these hardworking insects in the *Lasius* genus glittered like golden jewels in the sunlight when they emerged for a mating swarm from a piece of trunk sitting next to our front path one November afternoon. *Lasius* ants tend root-feeding aphids, herding them along underground from plant to plant, where the aphids can suck the juices that they later secrete as honeydew snacks for the ants to devour.

As they set up shop in dead wood and on the ground, these tiny creatures help break down organic matter and till the soil. The diverse roles of ants—as decomposers, aerators, seed dispersers, pollinators, predators, and plant protectors—add up to big impacts. "They are very powerful members of the community," says Buono, who has watched many an ant battle on her petri dishes and in the wild. "Ants act like sort of community regulators too. They can be very dominant organisms."

Watch ants in your garden, and it won't take long to understand how profoundly they shape their surroundings and are shaped by them in turn. In our habitat they haul seeds, bits of wood, butterfly wings, and any other organic object they can lift or drag. They form multilane expressways on the grapevines and Virginia creeper vines that crisscross the ground and ramble around the other plants, complete with underpasses, overpasses, spaghetti bowls, and hairpin off-ramps. They frequently stop to check out passersby, probably not so much with their eyes—most ants are thought to have poor vision—but with their antennae, which pick up on the subtlest scent differences and permit them to identify interlopers. They walk backward, a useful skill when coaxing heavy objects around innumerable obstacles. Ants even help relatives of our salt-seeking blue butterflies reach

To feed their colonies, ants carry away the dead bodies of cicadas, bees, butterflies, and many other insects.

adulthood. To enlist them as guards against predators and parasites, many caterpillars in the Lycaenidae family have stridulatory structures such as files and scrapers that "'call' the ants into service," wrote David Wagner in *Caterpillars of Eastern North America.* "The caterpillars' calls are substrate-borne, carried through the foodplants and other surfaces, so that ants walking nearby can detect the vibrations with their feet." Ants who heed the call are rewarded with a sugary substance secreted from the caterpillars' specialized dew patches and nectar glands.

The soil-tilling activities of desert leafcutter ants in Arizona benefit plant growth, as these industrious creatures construct subterranean farms under their nest mounds.

In the Sonoran Desert near Will's parents' house one November, we observe more of these diminutive insects' many talents, first spotting a leafcutter ant stand up on her back legs to hold an unwieldy, surfboard-shaped piece of dried leaf high enough in the air to avoid getting stuck in the sand. The desert wash is wide and open under the mesquite trees, so the view is less obscured here than in the dense understory of the eastern deciduous forest back home. As an ant construction crew hauls out a grain of sand at a time, it's easy to see how their underground activities stir up soil nutrients that benefit plants.

The massive undertaking will quickly result in a mound the circumference of a dinner plate and the shape of a volcanic crater. The grains look like boulders from an ant's perspective, and often when an ant appears to be struggling, a passerby stops to help carry the load and to set the building material carefully in place. Once the angled top of the mound is complete, the ants climb to the edge and toss their boulders down the side. Plink, plink, plink—one after the other, and though I can't hear them fall, I imagine an ant can.

Into the entrance of a nearby mound, where more ants haul sand grains up and out, foragers bring bits of fresh plant parts to be carried underground, waving them like banners at a holiday parade. Hidden from view are the farmers, feeding chewed-up leaves to a fungal crop that sustains the whole colony. Workers weed and prune this subterranean garden, which has been seeded by "starter fungi" their queens inherit from maternal nests—a precious gift that's often compared to the starter yeast passed down from mothers to their daughters for the making of sourdough bread.

I watch the ants until the sun sinks behind the saguaros and paints the air purple, grateful to go inside and have all the mushrooms and bread I want, made by a mother-in-law who passes her delicious ingredients and recipes down to me. I wonder: Which of our foods were made possible by ants prepping the soil? Which berries descended from bushes planted by coyotes, bears, or the mice who foraged for seeds in their scat? Which tomatoes and peppers have come to fruition through the hard work of wild bees? And I think of the ants back home, spending the winter where the land was cleared long ago and the trees are now shooting up again, where the violets and wild ginger take shelter under the new canopy and will soon beckon the ants to resurface from their underground hideaway and join them for the long warm season ahead. It might take several hundred years for these animal and plant partners to finish what they've begun. It's an ambitious project, but they're not alone. We are their allies, ensuring they have what they need to regenerate: the starter logs and starter leaves of a new, ant-filled, bee-buzzing, hummingbird-lit forest.

CHAPTER 4

The Touchscape

————

There is a crack, a crack in everything.
That's how the light gets in.
—Leonard Cohen

The clouds finally come without bluster, ushering in a slow-rolling wind that's more deliberate than all the atmospheric huffing and puffing that's teased us for days. Evening after evening for weeks, the baseless thunder has left us out to dry. As the land contracts, my world does too, and I focus mainly on keeping my growing habitat alive.

It's late July 2020, almost five months since I've hugged my parents and many weeks since the last rain. The breeze grazing my skin feels cooler this time, and the stagnant weight of high-pressure air seems to be lifting, a tangible signal for many animals that relief is on the way. But even the tree frogs seem tired of the sky's false alarms. Usually the first ones to pipe up at the slightest possibility of moisture, they remain silent as I head out the back door and down the path.

Closer to the pond, a sturdy bird flies past me and into a walnut tree. His beak and coloring differ from that of anyone I've seen in our habitat. I'm still at least twenty feet away, but he perches just long enough for me to lift my camera and quietly zoom in on his white belly and long, yellow beak. As heavy droplets start pinging my skin, the bird flies into the tulip trees across the path, and I head toward the house to find out more about my elusive new friend. A quick search of our field guides provides a photo match and a name: a yellow-billed cuckoo. Further reading reveals more interesting aliases: "Common folk names for this bird in the southern United States are rain crow and storm crow," reads an iNaturalist description. "These likely refer to the bird's habit of calling on hot days, often presaging rain or thunderstorms."

Something in me releases when I read this, cracking open a shell that has been hardening all summer. As the skies open up outside my office window, I do too. I cry with gratefulness for the rain and run outside to absorb the splash and jump in the puddles. I cry with joy for the rain crow who has let me into his world for even a brief moment. I cry in awe of the upending of everything I think I know each time an animal flies or crawls or leaps into view and tells me otherwise.

As my parched skin absorbs the cooling gifts, I'm transported to a distant forest of long ago, where I zigzag on toddler legs with my father across a trail, seeking refuge under the dense canopy when drizzle turns to deluge. We dash beneath the tallest tree to plot our next move. The sky booms. My dad squeezes my hand, and I look up to see if he shares my sense of foreboding. But he is smiling at me, his eyes twinkling. He says something funny, and we start laughing. I feel happy. Hand in hand, we make a break for it, dodging the downpour with the help of our tree friends, even though we're already dripping wet.

This is my first memory of being alive, in late July 1972, two months shy of my third birthday and exactly forty-eight years before I would meet the yellow-billed cuckoo. Decades later, that rain-soaked hike remains foundational to my worldview. The trees took care of me on that day, and so did my dad. It only makes sense that I've spent the rest of my life loving them back. Even on the worst of days, as the trees begin to outlive my human family, I take comfort and joy in their embrace.

The spring after I meet the rain crow in the walnut tree, I'm in the shock trauma unit, a place devoid of plants. The winds outside pick up as my father's heart winds down. I want to surround him with all the flowers in the world, the way he's done for me my whole life. In the end I've had to settle for a bouquet from my garden and sneak them to his hands because the hospital doesn't allow flowers. As the doctor calls his time of death, something catches my eye beyond the monitors. Pink flower petals and seeds float past the window. I'm fifty. My dad is eighty-four. It's 1:37 P.M., April 30, 2021. My dad is zero years old again, gone into the winds, floating with the next generation of trees.

I'll never know where the spring breezes carry those seeds beyond our fourth-floor view of downtown Baltimore. But I hope that at least one escaped the concrete to touch down among the roots and shade of an older tree, taking shelter from the stampedes just long enough to sprout, grow, and extend the same refuge to more seeds and birds and humans waiting for the storms to pass.

Hiding Places: Surrounded by Plants

The rain crow and I shared a rare moment, an encounter that hasn't been repeated. Many sources describe the clandestine ways of these shy animals, whose numbers are in decline throughout their range.

Elusive yellow-billed cuckoos are hard to spot, but this one flew into view just before a summer downpour.

Cuckoos are more adept than many other birds at eating spiny caterpillars, periodically ejecting their own stomach lining to get rid of the prickly bits.

"No bird is more secretive," North Carolina naturalist George Ellison wrote in the *Smoky Mountain News*. "Seldom leaving the shrouding foliage, the cuckoo sits motionless. When it does move, the cuckoo creeps about with furtive restraint. Seeing one is possible but unlikely. For the most part, this is a bird that you hear."

Impending rain can change the movement of birds. Even though their feathers and oil glands help them stay dry, low-pressure air makes it harder to gain lift for flying. When I happened upon the cuckoo, he'd probably been searching for a tree where he could wait out the rains, as my dad and I had done so many years before.

But there is something else about this bird's lifestyle that keeps him out of human sightlines and habitats. Yellow-billed cuckoos like to perch in places that many people are reluctant to approach, let alone nurture in their own yards. They live among dense thickets and shrubby woodland understory, and they like peaceful surroundings: research shows that yellow-billed cuckoos and nuthatches are ten times less likely to be found in areas with high-traffic noise than in quiet plots. Because of their largely hidden presence, cuckoos are generally not well studied, says Gabriel Foley, coordinator of the Maryland-D.C. Breeding Bird Atlas. "They're just very still birds, so they don't move around as much as a lot of other birds, and they like to be in cover," he says. "So they'll just sit there, they'll vocalize, and sometimes they'll kind of twitch their tail a little bit, and that's about it. If you do see them, especially when they're feeding, you'll see them walking along the limbs of trees, and they'll be picking off caterpillars."

Cuckoo diets are on the wild side, much more diverse than the buffet provided by birdfeeders. They eat caterpillars, especially hairy and spiny ones, but they also like cicadas, katydids, crickets, beetles, ants, spiders, elderberries, blackberries, wild grapes—not the stuff of a typical turf-laden landscape but the fruits of a more riotous, tightly woven, self-realized habitat, the kind that surrounds my home and shaded my parents on their outdoor visits during the first pandemic year.

Usually we all gathered under the sassafras growing by the patio, where ferns, wood asters, mayapples, jack-in-the-pulpit, and Virginia creeper mingled with mosses, fallen branches, and decaying leaves. Like the cuckoo's, my dad's voice was deep and strong, but it was not competitive, and sometimes we were unable to hear him speak above the din of the mowers and blowers next door. It was hard not to hold his hand during these visits, harder still to avoid touching him at all. He'd spent most of his life in labs and greenhouses, keeping flowers apart in pots to help them avoid disease transmission in mass production. As a plant pathologist, he studied how to prevent outbreaks. Now a new infectious virus had required us to do the same, isolating each branch of our family into our own walled containers. On the milder days when we could meet outside, we air-hugged from six feet away.

Our culture inflicts this type of social distancing on other living organisms even in the outdoors—to the point where allowing plants to grow near each other and animals to touch them has become a radical act. Landscapers and gardeners talk of "specimen" trees and "ornamental" shrubs and flowers as if they were inanimate objects made only for our own needs and pleasures, and in treating them this way we deprive the whole community, human and nonhuman alike. It's considered normal to force trees to stand lonely in mowed lawns

Once all turfgrass, our shaded patio area is now a mini-woodland that provides habitat for cuckoos and other wildlife. It also gave us a safe place to gather during the pandemic and was the scene of a celebration of my father's life after he died.

or in thick layers of the shredded carcasses of their friends. Shrubs trying to reach out to others don't get very far before their arms are cut off with pruning shears.

Ironically, while we've mastered this isolationist attitude toward plants and animals, our modern society is perfectly content to force unnatural crowding of single species for maximum profit. From the open wildlife markets of Asia to the windowless chicken factories and sprayed cornrows and pine plantations of North America, the

Wood frogs, the earliest to emerge in our habitat, attach egg masses to plants and twigs. Pristine ponds have no place in wild touchscapes, where frogs need still water to reproduce.

Water lilies give green frogs cover from hawks and intrusive humans.

effects of our global disregard for even the most basic needs of other beings—especially the need to both breathe and mingle—will always come back to haunt us. Crowded monocultures never end well, and reduced plant diversity has profound effects on human mental and physical health too, in ways far beyond the obvious: when researchers in Finland compared the health of children growing up in homes surrounded by native plants with that of kids in more conventional settings, they found that the ones closer to nature had more effective immune responses and an increased presence of protective bacteria on their hands. Such studies confirm that our relentless drive to live so separately from natural systems will only be to our detriment. As plant neurobiologist Stefano Mancuso notes in his manifesto *The Nation of Plants*, "We exist thanks to plants, and we exist only in their company. It behooves us to keep this idea clear at all times."

In our habitat, only the humans are required to social-distance during pandemics; everyone else continues to take up whatever space they want to, occupying different layers aboveground and below. Roots intertwine and connect through fungi in the soil, sharing water and nutrients. Branches of neighboring trees interlock and hold each other up. Grasses support tall wildflowers, helping them stay strong against the winds. Tall wildflowers risk standing out in the crowd as shy wallflowers blend in and hold their ground beneath, content to spread far and wide in the shadows of their more sun-seeking friends. Wood-frog mothers attach their egg masses to dried twigs leaning into the pond, hummingbirds nab soft seeds of golden ragwort to line their nests, crab spiders and caterpillars parachute away on silken threads of their own making, slugs create a telephone line of chemical cues in the slime they lay down to make the world more navigable, and snakes wander along textured surfaces where they can gain traction.

It's in these rich, connected touchscapes—the places where plants and animals meet unfettered by arbitrary notions of separation and isolation for the sake of aesthetics—that both the yellow-billed cuckoo and I are at home. The cuckoo needs the tactile companionship of the wild, the intact habitat of the tent caterpillars, whose silken nests nestle into the forked branches of black cherry trees. These moth larvae, in turn, also need to be surrounded by the natural fabric of their temporary houses. If they could speak for themselves, they might make a plea for a little more love and understanding: *We make a tent to take refuge from rains and cold weather and cuckoo birds, coming out only to eat or defend the nest. We share our bounty by leaving scent trails so our friends can follow in our footsteps to get to the best food supplies. We mean you and your trees no harm, but we have to eat and build our own shelters too. If you let us be, the leaves will return, growing long after we've turned into moths for a few days and perished. The trees are survivors.*

Like people coalescing in peace and protest, love and war, on the dance floor and on the battleground, tent caterpillars and their autumn counterparts—fall webworms—find strength and resources in their collective numbers. But their mass aggregations are threatening to those who want to dictate when and where animals and plants can gather. Our society is comfortable when we can put living beings in boxes and exert control over them—the hives of domesticated honeybees again come to mind—but when resourceful animals make their own shelter, we take umbrage. Despite the caterpillars' harmlessness to trees and to us, our sanitizing culture has deemed their homes

Tent caterpillars, an important food source for cuckoos, are especially fond of making their nests in the crotches of black cherry trees.

unsightly. Removal and death by pesticides are commonplace, a sad outcome for both the caterpillars and the cuckoo, who is one of their primary predators and devours as many as a hundred in a single meal. Even the cuckoos' reproductive timing and breeding locations are closely tied to the waxing and waning of these food supplies. "They're so unpredictable in where they'll be in any given year, just in terms of abundance or density but also when they'll nest. There aren't really any other species that are like that," says Foley. "They move around a fairly large region, and they're basically looking for these large insect outbreaks. Then as soon as they find one, that's when they'll start nesting." Males are good dads, helping build nests, taking their turns incubating eggs, and sharing feeding responsibilities of hatchlings and chicks before sending them off on their own into the forest.

By late July 2021, my own father has taken the prominent spot on my desk, smiling at me from a picture frame. Through the heavy air outside my window comes a plaintive song that's a cross between a hoot and a squeak, followed by a call reminiscent of a woodpecker drilling, a croaking thrum-and-tick sequence. The cuckoos are back, and as I spy the delectable fall webworm nest on the cherry tree, I realize that they've arrived just in time for the feast.

Self-Defense: Spineless but Not Stingless

August days bring dry skies. Instead of water, it's raining caterpillars, and one day I find a banded tussock moth caterpillar on my hat. Though all creatures are beautiful in their own way, this one is especially charismatic, his long white-and-black tufts making him look like a rock-star Muppet. I resist the urge to touch him, for both his sake and mine, and instead use a leaf to transfer him to a hickory tree where he can either keep feeding or prepare to make a cocoon.

Banded tussock moth caterpillars don't usually irritate the skin of other animals, but some other hairy species deliver a painful sting. Though caterpillar hairs often act as physical barriers to predators, sometimes the bristles—called setae—are also urticating, meaning they contain toxins, in the same way that stinging nettles (in the family Urticaceae) do. Plants and animals deploy surprisingly similar defense mechanisms for making themselves prickly to the touch; in Australia, researchers even recently identified neurotoxins in plants called stinging trees (*Dendrocnide* spp.) that resemble those found in spider venom.

Usually the venomous caterpillars I see are singletons going along their pokey way, like the fuzzy yellow American dagger moth caterpillar I've encountered crossing my front path. But one day while planting wild strawberries, I notice first one, then another, and then at least half a dozen more dazzling caterpillars descending the trunk of a redbud tree. They look dressed to the nines, all buttons and flash, with raised yellow and white dots splashed across a dark patch bordered by red on both ends. In the world of insects, those colors are a screaming warning light, and sure enough, closer inspection reveals long, silky hairs protruding from their bodies, with shorter, needlelike ones mixed in between.

These are the Sirens of the Soil, luring me to get closer to admire their beauty. Soon they'll bury themselves just underneath the surface, making cocoons for the winter before emerging in the spring as white flannel moths, glam-looking snow-white creatures with feathery collars who don't sting at all. Known scientifically as *Norape ovina*, they're gregarious feeders, emerging en masse to eat and eventually disperse into the ground. The second part of their Latin name means "like sheep," presumably referring either to their tendency to stick together or to the furry appearance of the adults.

Reading more about them, I learn that my instinct to look but not touch has saved me from painful blistering. But one animal's torture can be another's tantalizing treat, and it turns out that the white flannel moth caterpillars are a delicacy for the yellow-billed cuckoo, as I

Look but don't touch! The beautiful white flannel moth caterpillars, which emerge in large numbers in mid- and late summer on our redbud trees, are favorite snacks of cuckoos.

discovered when reading the Whatsthatbug.com account of a Virginia bird lover who described the "glorious infestation" on his honey locust tree:

> I am an avid birdwatcher and have contented myself with mostly listening for the shy, elusive cuckoos that appear in my yard every year. However, for the past week they have not been able to stay away from this tree and the buffet the caterpillars are providing—as many as

3 cuckoos hanging around gorging themselves just outside my door. I'm not concerned about the tree—just a bit of minor defoliation, and it's late in the season—but I sure hope that whatever bug this is decides to come back from now on so I can get such fantastic views of yellow-billed cuckoos! —Winston B.

Though many birds avoid caterpillars capable of stinging them or piercing their innards, yellow-billed and black-billed cuckoos are said to have special mechanisms for safely processing the spines. They roll the larvae back and forth and sometimes whack them on trees, presumably to remove at least some of the prickles before ingesting. But even when the spines end up sticking, the cuckoos just hit the eject button. "To get rid of the spines," notes the Cornell Lab of Ornithology, "they periodically shed the stomach lining, coughing it up in one giant pellet, similar to an owl."

If they escape the hungry mouths of cuckoos, some urticating caterpillars—like the larvae of white-marked tussock moths—incorporate their own stinging hairs into their cocoons. "They don't go to waste," notes Karin Burghardt, a University of Maryland assistant professor, and instead form a protective barrier of poison daggers. White-marked tussocks are also brave bungee-jumping adventurers. Wingless adult females can't fly, so they have to lay eggs in place. When the larvae emerge and leave the cocoon in search of food, "they make a silk line and basically balloon out to find new hosts," says Burghardt. As the tiny acrobats come in for a landing, sometimes they miss the mark; when I sat under a walnut, my arm became an airstrip for a tiny white-marked tussock caterpillar. In some species, such bold maneuvers are inspired by the presence of predators. To foil birds on the prowl for snacks, they drop down from trees and hang by their homespun threads until the threat has passed.

Shirtless and whistling, Will seems unaware of any of this as he helps me plant wildflowers beneath the redbud tree one afternoon. I warn him that he might want to get fully dressed. The day is sweltering, and he's reluctant—until he goes inside for a moment and sees a white flannel moth caterpillar on his hat. He runs excitedly outside, gently places his hat on the ground, and watches her inch her way across the path and toward the mini-woodland, where her new winter digs await.

Neighborhood Watches and Community Gatherings

Many animals and plants have evolved to be a bit prickly, and who can blame them? It's a tough world out there, and if you make like a porcupine and sink your quills into would-be attackers, all the better. If you're rooted to the ground, you might need a multifaceted defense system to ward off predators, especially the most destructive mammals of all: those pesky humans.

Horse nettle, a perennial in the nightshade family, has shown itself to be a worthy adversary of the anti-plant patrol, resisting herbicides and refusing to be cut down. Hack away at *Solanum carolinense*, and it'll just sprout new stems from its rhizomatous root reserves. Eat one of its fruits or leaves, and you'll be woefully sick at best, as implied by another of the plant's common names, "devil's potato." But you can't say you weren't warned; get too close to horse nettle, notes State Arboretum of Virginia curator T'ai Roulston, and it "grabs your

The prickliness and the toxic alkaloids of horse nettle deter browsers, but bumblebees rely heavily on the pollen in the plant's flowers.

ankles like a playful cat as it tears your pant legs, socks, and skin, scratching its name in a red and beaded script."

Sharp spines cover the stems and undersides of horse nettle leaves, protecting the plant from becoming dinner in the mouths of deer, rabbits, and many other mammals who are deterred by its toxic alkaloids. But that doesn't mean horse nettle is a miser—far from it. It shares its abundance with everyone from beetles and moth caterpillars to voles, raccoons, skunks, turkeys, bobwhites, wood ducks, and sparrows, who all dine on the fruit, apparently more immune to its toxins than we are. More than thirty insect species feed on horse nettle, including specialists who rely completely on the plant or closely related species. Bumblebees are especially fond of its white and purple flowers, as I discovered when horse nettle spread into a newly sunny area following my neighbor's removal of a row of pine trees. Walking along the path one early morning, I heard the distinctive sound of bees buzz pollinating before I saw them zipping around among the blooms, busily shaking pollen out of the bright yellow anthers to carry back to their nests.

Not everyone shares the bees' enchantment with horse nettles. Given the dominant culture's long history of maligning plants that don't overtly serve short-term human needs, I shouldn't have been surprised when a visiting native plant expert saw them popping up and pronounced them "scary." It stabs our skin, we can't eat it, and domesticated animals raised for food—including honeybees, who don't buzz pollinate—can't eat it either. Those three factors often doom fantastic wildlife plants, this one included, to top spots on "noxious weed" lists.

But in 2018, Roulston and his colleagues confirmed what the bees have long understood about the plant's value, in a study of bumblebee foraging habits at five sites within an hour's drive of Blandy Experimental Farm, the home of the arboretum where Roulston works. Of 112 types of pollen gathered by the bees, horse nettle was the clear favorite, making up between 19 and 38 percent of all pollen analyzed. "It turned out that at least two of the three most common bumblebee species are routinely using it to a great degree," says Roulston, "so it seems to be a pretty important resource." Its attractiveness to bees wasn't surprising to Roulston, who discovered during

Native field thistle feeds many animals, including goldfinches, while also protecting nearby vulnerable plants from being browsed before they can get established.

The flowers attract great spangled fritillary butterflies and other insects.

his graduate research that the pollen of plants in the Solanaceae family are near the top of the scale for protein content.

Though many landowners rip out such vital food sources and replace them with other pollinator plants, Roulston hopes his discoveries about horse nettle will encourage some to reconsider. But even if they don't, he's cheering on the plant for its resilience. "It is such a hardy weed that no matter how intensely people try to get rid of it, they're going to fail."

Horse nettle's vigorous defensiveness has hidden benefits for gardeners. Thanks to its prickly leaves and unpalatability to browsers, the plant shields fledgling coreopsis, echinacea, false sunflower, and rudbeckias in my habitat. These softer-to-the-touch species can be irresistible to our resident mammals when left out in the open. But when mingling with horse nettle or backed by native thistles, they enjoy the protection of natural caging and can mature enough to tolerate some nibbling.

Just as plants gain defense by association when growing near chemically fortified neighbors, they can also rely on the structural safeguards of thickets and thorns to avoid being eaten. It's a phenomenon seen in natural plant communities around the world. In a 2018 study in Kenya, researchers found a much higher sprouting and survival rate of understory savanna seedlings under the protective cover of acacia trees compared with those growing in more open spaces; the acacias' physical defenses provided a thorny barrier and also appeared to reduce the smaller plants' investment in chemical defenses, leaving them more energy for growth. On my visits to the southwestern United States, I often admire the baby saguaro cacti, still button-shaped, growing within the dense cover of sticky, unpalatable triangle-leaf bursage. In that case, the thorny plant is the one

Sometimes prickly plants need a head start too. On our visits to the desert Southwest, we see many saguaro cacti that have sprouted amid sticky triangle bursage, an important nurse plant that protects seedlings from extreme heat and herbivory.

being protected, while the resinous shrub is the protector. Triangle-leaf bursages are in the *Ambrosia* genus and are critical nurse plants, providing shade, adding nitrogen to the soil, and offering refuge from herbivores. One day the cacti will themselves become formidable, long-lived beacons for wildlife of the desert, but when they're still small and vulnerable, they need the embrace of other plants.

It's not that mammals will never eat prickly or tough-stemmed plants, but it can take longer to navigate to the tasty parts. In a study of Australian herbivores, researchers found that the greater the nutrient content in each bite, the less the animals needed to eat to satisfy their appetites. And just as the cuckoo bird has evolved to ingest spiny caterpillars and regurgitate the tricky parts, some herbivores have developed mechanical adaptations to structurally defended plants. In his book *The New Ecology*, Oswald Schmitz describes the "robust, crushing mouth parts" with which buffaloes and rhinoceroses consume tough leaves and the narrow, nimble mouths that give African antelopes the ability to move around thorns.

In my own habitat, many kinds of thorny plants offer protective services, shielding from herbivory the baby walnuts and redbuds sprouting amid their thickets. Wherever the black raspberries, Allegheny blackberries, and Virginia roses grow, we leave them, knowing they'll guard more vulnerable species—like young oak trees that are tasty to deer—while also providing flowers for bees, nesting sites for birds and rabbits, and berries for many creatures. But too many people still remove brambles because they feel offended by their prickly touch or consider them useless "undergrowth" (or sometimes "overgrowth"— whatever sounds the most negative in the moment, it seems).

In the distant past, forest caretakers appreciated thorns, which they referred to as "the mother of the oak," wrote Isabella Tree in *Wilding: The Return of Nature to a British Farm*. Shrubs were so sacrosanct that by 1768, anyone damaging thorny bushes and hollies in the New Forest, an ancient woodland in southern England, was subject to draconian punishment, including three months' forced labor and whiplashing. Used for centuries as common grazing and deer hunting grounds, the forest was heavily browsed, so forest officers threw acorns into the bushes, taking advantage of a natural barrier to protect sprouting saplings. The underappreciated understory plants thus nursed the young of species that would eventually tower over and sometimes overpower them.

In modern-day England, researchers have documented rapid reforestation on former agricultural lands bordering ancient forest at Monks Wood, a nature reserve in Cambridgeshire, thanks in part to the protective shrubs sown by thrushes and the acorns planted by Eurasian jays, gray squirrels, and wood mice. Following abandonment by farmers, return to dense woodland canopy took less than sixty years on one plot and less than twenty-five on another, a surprising outcome given the number of native roe deer and introduced Muntjac deer, says ecologist Richard Broughton, who led the research and set up cameras to track the number of deer. "They make trails through the shrubs and thorns and browse around the edges, but they don't get everywhere, and so plenty of young trees escape their attention," he says. "It's the pioneers of thorny hawthorn and bramble that make this possible, establishing first and growing quickly."

When land comes back to life on its own terms, without human interference, ecologists call it "passive rewilding," a self-willed process that can enhance biodiversity more than planned plantings. In a subsequent study, Broughton found that even former agricultural lands far from forests can take as little as three decades to grow into a rich mosaic of shrubland, wetland, and grassland that's buzzing with bees, butterflies, grasshoppers, dragonflies, and other insects. Surrounded by intensive agriculture and urbanized lands, the study site at Noddle Hill Nature Reserve in East Yorkshire is an oasis, home to song thrushes, European blackbirds, European robins and wrens, and many warblers. "The sound is spectacular, a medley all around

At Noddle Hill in East Yorkshire, England, passive rewilding of former agricultural land has created a rich mosaic of wetland, grassland, and shrubland that buzzes with life. Natural regeneration can lead to greater biodiversity than planned plantings.

you in the stillness of the morning, as a light mist lifts with the rising sun," says Broughton. "The birds sing throughout the day, but it is at its most intense and magical in the early morning."

Without the seed-dispersing Eurasian jays in the area or a nearby woodland with natural tree seed sources, Noddle Hill is likely to remain shrub-dominated for years to come. But a habitat in the middle stages of natural succession is not in purgatory. "Bramble gets a bad rap, probably because it's opportunistic and prickly, but it's a fantastic plant—not only as a nursery for protecting saplings from grazers, but also as a plant in its own right," notes Broughton, ticking off its many other benefits to wildlife and people. Often referred to as "scrubland," these transitional habitats may represent failure and loss in the minds of those who've watched them grow over lost crops, move in on docks, mines, and quarries of collapsed industries, or ramble through space that was desperately needed for intensive food-growing during the World War II era. But bramble-dominated areas are getting a rebrand, says Broughton, with conservationists encouraging the use of the word *shrubland* instead.

The sentiments against plant density—and the notion that they don't belong together unless we've planned it that way—also stem from practitioners of conventional forestry; the clear-cut-and-herbicide approach has long treated trees as individual warriors only out for themselves. In decades of research in the forests of British Columbia, ecologist Suzanne Simard found the opposite: when nitrogen-fixing alders are killed to release pines from perceived competition, a critical relationship is severed, and the pines that normally receive needed nitrogen from the alders—through an underground network of fine fungal filaments known as mycorrhizae—experience more threats to their survival. Similarly, when loggers cut birches with the goal of enhancing the growth of Douglas firs, the firs are more vulnerable to root disease and depleted of nutrients. By contrast, a self-organizing forest of interlocking roots, shared fungi, abundant seed banks, fallen nurse logs, and trees of many species and all ages is, as Simard has noted, "wired for healing."

Trees depend on one another not only for resource sharing but also for structural stability, staying much more grounded when they can interweave their roots. The ability of plants to work together to improve their environment and their own chances of survival can take many forms: shallow- and deeper-rooted species occupy different layers and can enhance soil structure, prevent erosion, and create a porous environment to soak up water. Even those with similar rooting depths might coexist by carving out their own niches, with one more adept at harnessing sunlight and another more able to obtain nutrients from shallow soil. Or they might time their growth spurts weeks or months apart to avoid competition. These cooperative arrangements are referred to as "functional complementarity" or "temporal complementarity," notes Schmitz. To me, though, they sound an awful lot like friendship.

Walking through a woodland on Maryland's Eastern Shore one fall afternoon, ecologist Joan Maloof and I come upon a beech tree that's about twenty-five years old. She is excited by the find. "The beech come in later than most. It's a sign of recovery in this forest," says the founder of the Old-Growth Forest Network, who helped save these 250 acres under our boots from development. "It takes forty years for it to start coming back after the forest has been completely cleared." But her delight is quickly overshadowed by the memory of a recent talk she attended in which a forester called beeches a "scourge" that should be cut down and sprayed.

In her book *Teaching the Trees*, Maloof has written of the abundant salamander life she encounters in beech forests and the beech-drop flowers that can live only at the feet of beech trees, whose roots provide sugars that the little plants are unable to make on their own. But the people cutting down beeches think there are more important things than salamanders and flowers. When beech roots are injured, Maloof explains, the trees put up new sprouts, sending foresters into a panic that they'll take space away from species considered more valuable on the lumber market. "But what damages the roots is the forestry equipment," Maloof says. "So they're causing this."

Left unmolested by heavy machinery, the beeches in Maloof's forest have no reason to fight for their lives so vigorously. "Look at this," she says, gesturing around the canopy. "We don't see any other beech tree around. They're not taking over." Mythology is pervasive in forestry, she notes, casting baseless aspersions on native trees like red maple and sweet gum simply because humans don't prefer to buy and sell and cut up their wood. How different would our stewardship practices look if we polled those with the most at stake, including my favorite rodents who stow away beechnuts and maple seeds among the brambling thickets, working together with the plants to reclaim the land?

Surfacing: Sculpting a Borderless World

A head pops out of the ground under the deck, nature's jack-in-the-box. The chipmunk seems to be around every corner, coming out of the woodwork of fallen branches and logs, the stonework of the retaining wall, the glade of ostrich ferns by the patio, and the underside of the air conditioner. Atypically for his usually shy and furtive species, he's even peeking out from behind the irises to greet me when I walk outside with my morning coffee. His favorite spot is the wall, where descending gray blocks make the perfect place to groom and show me his well-appointed underside, confirming that I've correctly guessed his gender. The flat expanse also provides a table for fine

Curious and bold, Mr. Chippie popped up to greet me on many spring mornings during the early days of the pandemic.

dining, and after Mr. Chippie has had his fill of snail breakfast, he leaves the shell behind as if he were at a bayside crab feast.

A few weeks later I spot a smaller chipmunk taking up residence in the front garden, devouring some good grub (or more precisely, grubs, of the beetle variety) in stumps, exploring pond rocks, and leaping to pluck berries straight from vines. Is it my imagination, or is it raining chipmunks too, in this summer of falling caterpillars and unpredictable storms? A scan of media reports confirms the latter, proclaiming a "banner year" in much of the East due to bumper crops of acorns over the previous two seasons. Their increased visibility is causing some level of consternation, but in spite of the hype about possible chipmunk invasions, "you really can't get overrun," says Penn State biology professor Carolyn Mahan. They're solitary and territorial, occupying a small home range, often only an acre or less, around their burrows. A cavalcade of chipmunks in one spot would indicate an unusual or unnatural circumstance, such as the presence of a bird feeder, which can draw rodents from all the surrounding territories like kids to an ice cream truck.

As my fondness grows for this industrious chippie who scurries back and forth along the wall, so do the mosses under his feet. My longing for softer green edges on the hardest of our hardscape, installed after stormwater pushed through rotting railroad ties and nearly turned our basement into a waterfall, is coming to fruition. *Entodon seductrix*, a fast-growing species that's as luxurious as its name implies, is clambering over the wall, atop a log, and down among the patio stones, where it mingles with cushiony brocade moss (*Hypnum imponens*). Mosses propagate by releasing spores into the wind, but sometimes they get a little help from animals like snails and slugs. Could it be that the chipster is also spreading mosses, laying out the green carpet that encourages his escargot snacks to make their mucusy way straight to his table?

He wouldn't be the only one. When botanist Robin Wall Kimmerer and one of her students tried to determine how a short-lived moss called *Dicranum flagellare* survived among more vigorous mosses in the Adirondacks, they systematically ruled out transport by wind, water, and slugs. The eureka moment came when a chipmunk crossed a log to have a go at one of their sandwiches. The next day, they temporarily captured a chipmunk and released him to scurry across a moss bed and white sticky paper. Sure enough, the cheeky chipster sprinkled "brood branches"—parts of the moss capable of cloning a new plant—as he ran. Watching more chipmunks cross logs and rocks provided additional clues as to how different species find their niches: "We noticed that when they came to a halt little bits of moss were kicked up from the surface, like gravel spun out by a hard-braking car," writes Kimmerer in *Gathering Moss*. The resulting "potholes" were just the right size for *D. flagellare* to drop down off the chipmunk and mingle with more widespread sister species.

Mosses are adventurous in finding their own homes, their spores even traveling overseas on global winds. But clearly animals can have more of a role in this dispersal than once thought. Researchers have found that another common bryophyte, fire moss, emits scents that attract springtails, tiny invertebrates who then spread the moss's sperm. The result is increased fertilization, a phenomenon that's been likened to the relationship among flowering plants and pollinators.

By the next spring, *Entodon seductrix* is patchy and full of gaps. A nighttime wildlife camera confirms why: busy bird parents have been plucking large patches to use in their nest construction. Eastern phoebes, Carolina wrens, orioles, and chickadees are among those who rely on the soft padding to protect their young. The chipmunks line their burrows with it too, as do voles, flying squirrels, and bears. Moss lawns provide refuge to many of the smallest creatures, including ants, spiders, and firefly nymphs, who find needed moisture and humidity in mossy environments.

Despite the importance of moss to so many animals, this welcoming touchscape, where snails glide along and chipmunks lie in wait

The aptly named *Entodon seductrix* moss softens the hard edges of our landscape.

In early spring, bald patches start to appear on our retaining wall. A wildlife camera caught the culprits: birds gathering moss for their nests.

to meet them, is often destroyed. I've met homeowners in the mid-Atlantic who've been fined for daring to nurture it, and I've seen entire mossy habitats obliterated elsewhere. In Hawaii, a land with a long history of foreign invasion and an overwhelming number of introduced species, mosses cling for dear life to rocks facing the crashing sea, while sprinklers behind them water acres of freshly laid sod for new subdivisions. The ancient plants thrive mainly in forgotten pockets: oceanside boulders too steep to climb, strip mall walls too lowly to attract notice. They grow in the increasingly narrow spaces between golf courses and resorts, on rocks and hard places where volcanic terrain appears to be the only barrier left to development. The Hawaiian expression *Limua ka moku* translates to "The land is moss-covered," but as one dictionary notes, it suggests something sadder about the effects of thoughtless human expansion and volatility on the smallest organisms: "There is peace in the land, and no wars to disturb it."

When the birds disturb the mosses on the stones and walls of our patio, it takes only a few weeks to fill in again, much to the delight of Mr. Chippie, who spreads belly-flop style across the wall one afternoon, resting atop his green fuzzy tower. As I watch him navigate two worlds, diving into the subterranean burrow among the wild geraniums one day and climbing trees the next, I realize that to chipmunks, it's all one world: a single dynamic place with no line separating above from below. Their domain is the length and width of the trees, and they touch every part of it, from the roots to the tips, starting with the burrows, which are often made from spots where roots leave hollow spaces after trees have died.

Chipmunks are creatures of the trees in every way, eating the seeds and nuts of maples, oaks, beeches, and hickories, and storing large stashes for the winter. They like to mate in the privacy of fallen logs, which offer protection from predators and competitors. They use crushed leaves in their nests, and as noted by Lang Elliott in his delightful 1978 graduate thesis on the mating and foraging habits of chipmunks, they also rely on fallen leaves to provide a safety net. "My observations of crown foraging during the autumn of 1973 indicate that chipmunks are not very finely adapted for arboreal maneuvering," he wrote diplomatically in his 106-page tome exploring chipmunks' natural history. Because beech bark was too smooth for them to get a grip, the animals used the rough bark of maples to climb to the canopy, where they then had to figure out how to make their way to the beechnuts. Once their pouches were filled with nuts, they also needed to adeptly navigate their way back to solid ground again. "I observed a total of four individuals fall out of crowns at heights of approximately 18 m.," Elliott wrote. "On four other occasions, I heard the unmistakable thumps of falling chipmunks hitting the ground and I visually located them just after their falls."

Recalling the scene almost fifty years later, Elliott still remembers how worried he was when his most-studied chippie slipped while foraging in the beech trees, likely tripped up by the smooth bark. "She came to and she was twitching in one leg, going in circles. And I'm watching and I'm like, this is not good news," he says. "She was my favorite. But then finally she was upright and carried on and weaned her young." Though indirectly, it was the trees that came to the rescue, creating cushioned safety nets on the ground all around their trunks. "None of the chipmunks appeared seriously injured," wrote Elliott, "but all had landed in the soft leaf litter."

For all that trees give chipmunks, it might seem at first to be a one-way exchange. But chipmunks' habit of occasional scatter-hoarding,

Chipmunks are creatures of the trees, eating nuts, burrowing in the hollowed-out soil of old roots, using leaves to cushion their underground homes, and foraging for beetle larvae in stumps and logs.

Mole activity creates a welcoming substrate for new plants, including hard-to-grow grape ferns.

involving hiding nuts and seeds in temporary stashes, inevitably plants new trees. And recent research indicates that chipmunks even play a vital role in connecting those trees with the resources they need to grow and thrive.

This new clue helps me unravel a mystery that has emerged in the shade of our silver maple. Among the Appalachian sedges, Virginia creeper, barren strawberries, American hollies, and Eastern red cedars sprouting around the roots, gently undulating molehills have come alive with the fronds of grape ferns. These plants are neither grapes nor ferns, though they look a bit like both, with lacy leaves and large, lime-green spore clusters. They're new to our habitat, and as far as I know, new to our whole community. And they seem to be following directly in the moles' footsteps, sprouting atop and along the sides of several mounds the moles have created during their many excavations.

Grape ferns are all but impossible to intentionally cultivate; you can't buy them at a nursery because no one has figured out how to replicate the mysterious circumstances required. Spores need weeks of darkness, enveloped in soil, to germinate underground. Roots develop before leaves, so no chlorophyll exists to help spin sunlight into sugars. In the absence of photosynthesis, the grape fern's food supply comes from partners underground: mycorrhizal fungi penetrate the plant's cells to deliver nutrients gleaned from other species, likely nearby flowering plants and trees. The fungal network acts like a grocery service, picking up and delivering needed goods throughout the community in exchange for sugars from the plants.

Given their mysterious ways and finicky requirements, why did the grape ferns show up at the front of our property by a busy road, where mowed lawn dominated the land until just a few years ago?

The answer is a mystery to the scientists I ask too. "That would be a great study," says one ecologist, musing that maybe moles had a role all along but escaped everyone's notice. Others respond that my guess is as good as theirs. Eventually I happen upon the work of Ryan Stephens, a wildlife ecologist in New Hampshire who spends many of his days studying the influences of small mammals on forest dynamics. When I contact him, he tells me right away that he knows nothing about grape ferns. But his research may help connect some of the dots.

By examining the scat of small mammals, Stephens has identified the significant role of chipmunks and mice in the dispersal of mycorrhizal fungi that nurture plants, a discovery that started with a walk in the woods. The same excavations that frustrate many gardeners intrigued Stephens when he first noticed them on the ground among the hemlocks. Why would animals be wasting time digging small holes to nowhere? "At first I thought the mammals were really dumb," he jokes. But eventually it clicked: the little creatures of the forest had their eyes on the truffle prize, sniffing out the fruiting bodies of ectomycorrhizal fungi, which grow between and around the roots of many trees. "In Europe, truffles are evolved for dispersal with things like wild boar, and they're really large," Stephens says. "In this region of the United States, most of the truffles have evolved with smaller mammals." As such, they can be about the size of a little potato and sometimes much smaller than that, at only a few millimeters. They can also be quite odiferous, smelling a bit like basil or a lot like a combination of road tar and garlic. Stephens has studied fungi in such detail that in the process, he's even discovered five previously unrecorded and unnamed *Elaphomyces* species.

When ecologist Ryan Stephens wondered why small mammals were digging holes to nowhere in a New Hampshire forest, his investigations led to a fascinating discovery: they were seeking *Elaphomyces verruculosus* and other strong-smelling truffles.

When mice, voles, chipmunks, and other small mammals dine on truffles, they nurture forest growth by dispersing fungal spores in their scat.

Other kinds of fungi, known as arbuscular or endomycorrhizal, penetrate root cells and are associated with grasses and forbs, like the grape ferns in my habitat, as well as some trees, like the silver maple above them. While they don't produce truffles, they do have aggregates of spores, called sporocarps, around the roots. Small mammals can also detect these tasty tidbits as they scurry along the soil surface. "They have a much better sense of things than we do," says Stephens.

Researchers in the Pacific Northwest have long known that red-backed voles, specialists who eat primarily fungi, have a key role in dispersal. But Stephens's studies have illuminated the importance of mammals with broader diets. When their populations increase following beech tree masting, generalists such as chipmunks and deer mice can disperse an even greater number of fungal species than red-backed voles. They often cover more ground and more habitats while foraging, and they do so at an optimal time when new seedlings are sprouting on the forest floor. Even in clear-cut patches, Stephens found that meadow voles and meadow jumping mice are abundant dispersers of arbuscular mycorrhizal fungi, suggesting their activities could be critical to forest regeneration. "I didn't expect them to have as much fungi or really much spores at all in their scat," says Stephens, noting the seeming barrenness of the plots. "So I was surprised when I started looking through their scat that they had pretty decent spore loads—as much as some of the other species."

Back in Maryland, did the furry earth movers prep the land for the growth of both the grape ferns and the fungi they require? Were the grape fern spores brought in on the feet or fur or feces of small mammals, the spores' thick walls enabling them to pass through an animal's gut intact? It can take years for grape ferns to make an appearance above ground, but the spores may have been in the seedbank from long ago, just needing a little help from tunneling mammals to move closer to the surface. Or deer could have eaten grape ferns elsewhere and pooped out the spores under the maple. In the latter case, a whole chain of events may have been triggered: moles could have covered the spores with soil, giving them needed darkness to germinate. And voles and chipmunks, who treat mole tunnels like highways, may have added or spread the final ingredient in their scat: spores of the grape ferns' mutualistic fungal partners.

Through all their tilling, tunneling, and burrowing, animals sculpt the land. They touch every part of it: the soil, logs, stumps, and leaves are their home, and they are much better than we are at creatively using whatever is on hand. Moles make tiny hills and valleys, a microtopography that allows mosses to grow on surfaces just tall enough to survive above the leaf layer. Shrews, voles, and chipmunks might push up a plant, chew on a root, or spill out some soil onto the sidewalk, but these are part of the process, not an end result. The end result is always more beginnings: nests where newborn birds are cradled in moss gathered from molehills left to evolve and devolve; fresh fronds of grape ferns who've taken their sweet time gathering strength from the underground community. Once the plants finally raise their arms to join their friends above the surface, they can grow for decades.

The more I learn, the more I know that my efforts pale in comparison with those of the chipmunks, the fungi, the mosses, the moles, and the trees, who mingle and chatter continuously in sensory languages that we can barely begin to decipher. Even flower petals floating in the spring breeze—like those I watched outside my dad's hospital window—might signal chipmunks about impending food supplies. The emergence of tree buds may play a role in the seventeen-year cicada life cycle too; in a study of cicadas' timekeeping mechanisms, when scientists manipulated trees to bloom twice in one season, the insects responded accordingly and emerged a year early. What feels ethereal to us gives practical clues to animals whose lives depend on seasonal changes, as they try to judge how abundant or sparse the impending bounty will be, adjusting their preparations accordingly for future gains and losses.

Mud Masons and Leaf Recyclers: Mining the Soft Edges

Late in the season, I haul woodchips to make paths, apologizing repeatedly to the tree whose life has been reduced to this. We've gratefully accepted our neighbor's offer to have his maple's chopped-up corpse dumped onto our driveway, but doing so has made me feel complicit in her demise. No amount of reasoning could persuade our friend to spare the tree; the surface roots disrupted his lawn mowing. While we have gotten rid of our lawn (and mower) to avoid disturbing roots and shoots and animals in our habitat, some people in our community are doing the opposite—getting rid of trees to save lawn.

Consolation comes sooner than expected, when one of my wilder neighbors figures out how to make new life out of the unnecessary loss. Kneeling in the garden while talking on the phone one evening, I feel the presence of someone behind me and turn to see an Eastern box turtle making her way determinedly down the new path edging the meadow. She checks out one grassy patch after another before

An Eastern box turtle mama laid eggs in the memorial garden I created for my father. The telltale scar on her shell helped us recognize her as an old friend.

Squirrels insulate their nests with fallen leaves, creating habitat for litter moths. Bumblebees sometimes reuse old squirrel nests too.

finally settling on the slightly elevated bank of a wildflower border. Next to the cardinal flowers, she digs first through fallen leaves and woodchips and then sinks her back legs into the soil to further excavate. Eventually it's too dark to watch her anymore, but when I return the next morning, she has put everything back in place, leaving no trace of her labors.

Over the next two weeks, I see her digging two more nests, one at the edge of a new memorial garden I've just created in honor of my dad. If I didn't know better, I might think the turtle is following me. At the very least, it seems she's attracted to my path making: the newly dug soil and the cover created by decaying organic matter make a perfect substrate.

Spent plants take on a life of their own—and sometimes many lives. Squirrel nests not only make a cozy spot for bumblebee colonies but, as Burghardt discovered when she moved to her neighborhood near the University of Maryland, these twig-and-leaf condos are also valuable real estate for litter moth caterpillars. "That first summer, I started coming across these squirrel nests that have fallen out of trees," Burghardt recalls. The leaves were skeletonized, creating a lacelike effect, so Burghardt brought the nests to her lab to examine them. "And basically, there were hundreds of these litter moths."

Setting up insect-rearing tents in her yard, she observed some of the nests all winter and found caterpillars feeding on the dead leaves throughout the cold season. It takes about two months for the caterpillars to break the leaves down, converting an entire nest into mostly frass—"a really nice fertilizer," says Burghardt. Not only do squirrels' choice of construction materials appeal to the moth caterpillars—staying damp in the center and creating an attractive microenvironment—but also, Burghardt theorizes, their chosen locations could confer protection from the onslaught of neatnik bipeds: "They might be safer up there from removal by humans."

Down on the ground, animals find uses for damp leaves in other unexpected ways. Watching a mass toad emergence one spring, I see a male hop atop a rainwater-filled leaf, thrust his hindlegs back, and shimmy from side to side as if grooving to some smooth froggie jazz that only he can hear. His bebopping more likely serves an essential purpose: many frogs, including American toads, absorb water through their thin belly skin in an area near the pelvic region known as a "seat patch."

Hard-packed earth—created by leaf removal, tilling, heavy machinery, and an absence of plants—lessens such opportunities for countless creatures. It can even negatively affect caterpillars trying to head below the surface. At Georgetown University, biology professor Martha Weiss's lab is studying the effect of packed earth on moth species that pupate by burrowing. "If your soil is too compacted, they can't get down there very far, or it will take them a lot longer," she says. The extra effort could make them more vulnerable to predation.

Tunneling mammals provide a solution to this problem that rivals that of even the best gardener, creating unexpected habitat for many types of invertebrates. Studying the nesting sites of the endangered rusty-patched bumblebee in urban and suburban areas, researchers in the Midwest discovered that one colony had made itself at home in what appeared to be an old chipmunk burrow. Among the wild geraniums under our deck, our female chippie friend's obsession with adjusting her burrow entrance has created prime habitat for cicada killer wasps, who excavate their nests in the loosened soil—a home within a home. Benign toward humans, the wasps use their stingers to prey upon annual cicadas, whom they paralyze and store as food for their larvae. During her foraging trips, a mother cicada killer wasp is impossible to miss as she engages in epic battles to overwhelm her prey. The piercing screams of cicadas are painful to hear, especially if you have a fondness for these musical gentle giants. But the wasp is apparently immune to cicada sounds, writes Eric Eaton, instead relying on its sense of touch. "Deaf to the cicada's call, but sensitive to vibrations," Eaton notes in *Wasps: The Astonishing Diversity of a Misunderstood Insect*, "she gleans limbs of trees and other likely perches, eventually blundering into a cicada."

Like the chipmunk, Will and I have inadvertently created wasp habitat through a digging project of our own. One afternoon by the pond, where we've piled unearthed soil on the banks, I hear a high-pitched drilling, quiet but intense. At first the whirr reminds me of bumblebees buzz pollinating. But a closer look reveals that these sounds of industry are coming from one of nature's most diminutive architects: an organ pipe mud dauber wasp. She's using her mandibles to dig into wet clay and form a mud ball, which she then picks up with her front legs and carries off. It all happens in a flash, and she's back within minutes to repeat the process.

My mental recall of buzz pollination by bees was no coincidence: mud dauber wasps use a similar mechanism to mine the soil, turning into "musical masons," writes Justin Schmidt in *The Sting of the Wild*, by contracting their thoracic flight muscles to vibrate their head and mandibles. A study of black-and-yellow mud dauber wasps found that they apply different frequencies for different tasks; mud gathering generates high-frequency sound, while nest plastering emits sound at a lower frequency. Mining bees who excavate sand also use

Nothing is wasted in nature, where animals often make homes within homes. This leafcutter bee in the Florida garden of my friend, bee advocate Laura Langlois Zurro, navigated through a spider web inside a decayed plant stalk that was blowing in the wind. The bee hovered patiently until she could get past the sticky web and line her nest with petals of partridge pea flowers.

this technique when bringing pollen and nectar back to their nests. "Because their nest entrance just collapses when they leave, they will sonicate head first down through the loose sand to get into their burrow," says Heather Holm, the author of several pollinator books, including, most recently, *Wasps: Their Biology, Diversity, and Role as Beneficial Insects and Pollinators of Native Plants.* As ancestors of bees, wasps may have passed on this trait, says Holm, or the ability to sonicate may have evolved separately in bees—another mystery that has yet to be explored.

Ideal locations for nests of organ pipe mud dauber wasps are shady spots protected from rainfall, near mud and forest. In the wild, that might be a hole in a tree; in my own habitat, it's the underside of our deck. For as long as we've lived at our house, organ pipe mud dauber wasp nests have graced the deck beams above the entrance to our basement, but they are so unobtrusive that you have to look up and pay close attention to see a wasp at work. This time we finally catch one in action, following her back and forth from the wet clay patch on the bank of our pond to her deck lair. Watching her stretch mud balls out, elongating her organ pipe nest a little more with each trip, I admire the wasp's artistry and dedication: as she creates cells for eggs within the tube, she also catches and paralyzes spiders, stuffing them into each cell so her wasp babies will have something to eat when they hatch.

During the hours spent observing nest construction over several days, I'm surprised to see the head of another wasp peeking out of the tube, sometimes quickly retreating and sometimes chasing away other wasps. Organ pipe mud dauber wasps don't aggregate in colonies; it's one of the reasons they're gentle around people, since they have no large group or long-term nest-building activities to defend. But that

Organ pipe mud dauber wasps use their mandibles to mine wet clay and carry the mudballs to their nests, where they stretch them around to elongate the tubes—often under a deck or a protective overhang.

doesn't mean they're completely solitary. Nest creation is a family affair, and the second wasp, it turns out, is a dedicated dad. Male organ pipe mud dauber wasps stay in the nest to guard larvae while the moms collect building materials. Sometimes they even help with construction, but their main role is protection. Without their vigilance, other mud dauber wasps might try to claim the nest as their own.

The hovering dads also have to be on the lookout for predators and parasitoids, including flies and other wasp species. While observing the nest building, I see a beautiful and persistent cuckoo wasp try repeatedly to find a secret passageway into the nest. She doesn't succeed; the father mud dauber is on high alert and chases her away. But if cuckoo wasps manage to sneak into the pipes and lay eggs, their progeny will later kill the baby mud daubers and then eat their spidery provisions.

This strategy doesn't seem like a neighborly way to raise a family, but I can't help feeling sorry for the mama cuckoo wasp: it must be difficult to have to engage in such covert operations just to find a home for her young. I can't ponder the odd behaviors wrought by evolution for long, though. Soon enough, a rusty spider wasp comes into view, and this one carries a heavy load, dragging along a hapless spider destined to become a meal. My heart goes out to the little spider even as I reason that wasps need to eat too. But once again, the arthropods have no time for such sentiments. During a brief moment when I turn away to record the spider's sad demise, one of his behemoth cousins, a dark fishing spider, comes to level the playing field, parking herself right underneath the mud dauber wasp nest.

Dark fishing spider mothers are also dedicated parents, carrying their egg sacs around in their mandibles and pedipalps until the spiderlings are ready to emerge; I've gotten a peek at these shy, protective moms a few times in the garden as they scurry away to safety. They're in the nursery web spider family, so called because the mothers create a tent, attach their egg sacs inside when they're about to hatch, and guard over the spiderlings until they disperse after their first molt. Unlike web-spinning spiders, who locate prey more by feeling vibrations than through eyesight, the dark fishing spider relies on vision to chase and pounce on victims. The new arrival under the deck stays still for a long time, and if she eventually catches her quarry, I'm not there to see it. I suspect our wasp family survives, though. Just a few days later, they've laid down a second pipe, still hard at work on soil mining, nest building, and protecting and providing for the next generation.

Climbing and Falling

Landscape designers often tout the importance of creating a sense of place to make humans feel at home. But our wild friends already know exactly where they are. Who has a better sense of place than the animals and plants whose whole bodies touch the earth, who lie down with the rocks and the sand and rise up with the stems and the bark? Who knows the location of every mayapple and wild strawberry better than the box turtle who travels the same few acres for decades? Who understands the contours of the fallen leaves and twigs more than the slug who glides along them each night, forging her own slippery trail to smooth over the rough spots of her journey? Who among us has scoped out the best way to climb a wall sideways and without legs, wrapping our underbellies around every angle while muscling our way silently forward along the narrow ledges, the way a snake does? Who is more grounded in her surroundings, more rooted in her reality, than the tree who holds out her arms to the winds and absorbs every storm at her feet?

As a generalist species, we humans have the biological capacity to make our homes and find our food practically anywhere in the world. But how familiar are we, really, with those who are more tied to the land at our doorsteps? What do we know of the life of a dying ash tree who has seen and felt so much, like the one in my backyard who watches over the beetles scurrying about above her roots, hears the circling red-tailed hawks above her canopy, and holds the bluebirds and squirrels in her weakening limbs? For me, the trees and all the life they nurture don't just confer a sense of place. They *are* the place. They are my home, and the least I can do is try to get to know them before it's too late.

Once the tallest plant on our initially sparse land, the lone ash tree began releasing her burdens a few years ago whenever the wind blew too hard, leaf by leaf, twig by twig, and then heavy branch by heavy branch. Her departure started not with the emerald ash borer, the insect that has sent many of her kind to their doom, but with a large fracture that split her trunk almost in two—an injury my father pointed out one summer while walking in the garden with me. In spite of her wound, the tree stood tall for a few more years, still cradling all the creatures of our mini-forest. One season, when she had no leaves left to give, she offered bits of her lichen coat to hummingbirds decorating their nests.

After my dad discovered the fissure, a kind arborist spent hours admiring the tree, climbing into the canopy and walking into the back meadow to consider her from different angles. He gave us two estimates: one for adding reinforcing cables to provide extra stability in the short term and one for cutting and grinding the ash into wood chips. The latter option would be drastic for the life around the tree, he warned, gesturing toward the surrounding riot of flowers and grasses. "These plants will go into shock with all that sudden light." In the end, he added a single loose cable to try to hold the trunk together just a little bit longer, reminding me of the strategies of my mom's surgeons, who wrapped a cable around her crumbling hip bones to keep her upright and a wire into her heart to steady her rhythm.

Old dying trees, lovingly termed "mother trees" by Simard, can pass nutrients through underground mycorrhizal fungi to surrounding trees throughout the forest, leaving a priceless legacy for the next generations. Their slow breakdown also enriches the soil, creating fertile ground for new arrivals. As the matriarch of our backyard grew thin, dropping more brittle branches every year, the world below her gathered strength. Each summer among the ostrich ferns, golden ragworts, and black cohosh already at the base, new plants arrived to greet her—first pokeweeds and Virginia creeper, later spicebushes and sassafras trees, and then walnuts, black cherries, and pin oaks. The plants formed a large circle around the old lady, protecting her from winds and casting shade in new places. In the surrounding gardens, the wildflowers and saplings, long situated tenuously just beyond the sun's brightest rays, burst forth from the receding shadows. The tree's canopy shrank as theirs expanded, inviting tulip trees and sweetgums, redbuds and maples. The serviceberries and sweetbay magnolia that once struggled along for more sunshine shot up and out, coming into the world with more energy as fleabanes and woodland sedges and nimble will grasses spread underneath.

Some of the plants competed for light and space; some collaborated. Together they formed a thriving community, separately from the plans I once had for them and far more beautifully than I could have anticipated. Where black raspberries staked out new spots, meandering around the tree trunk, they held together large webs of spiders. Structure is essential for web construction; in flattened, two-layered landscapes that contain only turfgrass and tree canopy, there is nothing for spiders to hang on to, no walls to contain their homes and stringy pantries. The loss of their webs is a loss to the food web as a whole, as spiders are not only important predators but also prey, often composing almost the entire diet of newborn birds like chickadees, who also now nest among us.

Recently it became too dangerous to walk beneath the tree anymore, so the kind arborist came back and cut the remaining branches, leaving them in piles that we could distribute around our habitat for birds to peck at and foxes to den under. The tree is now a wildlife snag, her twenty-foot trunk and branches still home to her animal

When the mother tree of our habitat became too dangerous to walk under, an arborist helped us turn her into a wildlife snag, where woodpeckers drill, hawks perch, and seedlings of new plants continue to sprout in her wake.

friends, her roots still weaving through the roots of her many green companions. The drying wood is strong, the arborist assures me, and will remain so for years to come, even as beetles and fungi start to soften the edges and woodpeckers begin drilling cavities where generations of bird families will nest. She is no longer a fall risk, so I can keep close company with her again. Though I don't really know how she experiences the world, I can sit with her and try to understand, staying still enough to feel the winds of the wings of spicebush swallowtail butterflies as they fly low near her base and nearly graze my legs, courting in the cardinal flowers and laying eggs on the spice-bushes. I can pick flowers from her shadows to make a bouquet for my own mother, in gratitude for all the gifts she gives me even when the surgical wires and bone cement holding her hips and back together have started to fray and crumble too. And I can remember what it was like to fall for the first time into the cool and forgiving earth.

I'm four years old, and it's still dark, but I'm wide awake in the top compartment of my family's pop-up camper. The damp air accentuates the sweet mustiness of the brown-and-orange-flowered fabric covering the thin foam mattress beneath me, a scent of water mixed with tapestry that never quite dries but isn't moldy either. Through the blue plastic ventilation holes of the pop-up walls I hear crickets and smell earth, and I grow restless for the day to start.

My sister doesn't share my anticipation, so I poke her, unaware that irritating people is not an endearing strategy for getting them to hang out with you. "Stop it!" she snaps, pushing my hand off and rolling away from me. To spite her, I roll away in protest too, loudly and as far as I can to the other side.

The metal snaps holding our road-weary home together weren't designed to contain the manifest emotions of a willful child, and I tumble through a dark tunnel, down, down, down—as my dad would eventually fall at a curb, forty-five years later, hitting his head on the concrete; as my mom would fall in the garden that same spring, lying there for fifteen minutes before anyone realized she was missing; as Will would still later fall one scary early spring morning, when a torn muscle caused his leg to give out. At some point we all fall, and if we're lucky, like Will and my mom were, we get up and keep going with the help of our families and friends. If we're really lucky, like the chipmunks and I, we are completely unscathed, thanks to the soft layers created by endless breakdowns and renewals of rising and falling trees.

I lie in the roiling mud, astounded to be alive one second and wailing for my mother the next, frightened to be out in a world that might as well have been another planet without her. But the scare lasts only a second before she's there with her arms outstretched, smiling, fussing over me, comforting me, carrying me inside like a mama squirrel relocating her babies, stooping at the hook-up sink with washcloths and Wet Ones to clean me up, marveling at how unmuddy I am, telling me everything is OK and that it isn't my fault that I fell, that the buttons must have been loose, that it would be a good day today in the welcoming forest.

CHAPTER 5

The Sightscape

One way to open your eyes is to ask yourself,
"What if I had never seen this before?
What if I knew I would never see it again?"
—Rachel Carson, *Silent Spring*

Calling boisterously from his perch on a maple branch, the Carolina wren declared his proud new homeownership. This was his garden now, the perfect place to settle down with his mate and raise their growing family.

From our chairs on the driveway, my sister, Janet, and I reveled in his territorial music, a kind of victory song for us too. The day before, the Maryland legislature had codified her right—and the right of people across the state—to grow gardens for bees, butterflies, birds, and other wildlife. Her four-year battle with her homeowners association had planted the seed for a much larger fight, and now it was time to celebrate the new law of the land.

As we raised our glasses to toast one big leap forward for local wildlife and the gardens they rely on, the birds were just getting started on their next project. Carolina wren couples are devoted parents, staying together year-round and sometimes mating for life. They aren't particular about their real estate, as long as it's protected from

Moss is prime home-decorating material for Carolina wrens, who gather it for their nests from molehills, logs, and walls.

An HOA board spent about a hundred thousand dollars trying to destroy my sister's butterfly garden in favor of turfgrass. They did not succeed.

the elements: a tree cavity, the roots of an upturned shrub, a stump, a patch of dense vines. If no such spots are available, the creative little birds make do with a flowerpot, a mailbox, a space behind the cushion of a chair, or, as at my house once, the grill of an old truck that hadn't been driven for a while.

The wrens don't ask for much, and they have their priorities straight. They recycle, fashioning homes for their young from strips of bark, dried grasses, fallen leaves, mosses, feathers, snake skins, pine needles, sticks, and anything else that might keep fragile chicks cradled and warm. They live in harmony with plants, protecting them from insects who would devour their leaves and stems—caterpillars, beetles, true bugs, grasshoppers, and many others—by feeding this ravenous crew to their young.

But if my sister's neighbor had gotten his way, most of the wrens' housing construction materials would have disappeared, and their grocery shelves would be empty. Despite the low demands and helpful ways of these hardworking birds, they were once unwelcome in Janet's community, where one resident took it upon himself to declare turfgrass the only acceptable plant and to decry the presence of animals as verboten. For years he influenced the HOA board president and a hired lawyer to decree the same, and this small group of unreasonable men spent about a hundred thousand dollars of the community's money trying to destroy the garden of my sister and her family—and the home of the wrens. In a series of bullying letters, the HOA's contracted law firm wrote that a garden "without the use of pesticides in which they have maintained 'native plants' to provide food for birds, bees, and other insects and animals" is "completely contrary to the overall design scheme for the Association, which is a planned development. Lots within the Association are intended to be uniform in design and character with manicured yards and green grass for lawns." The attorney used quotes around words and concepts he apparently viewed as suspicious, such as "garden," and wrote disparagingly of Janet and her family's "environmentally sensitive agenda."

The ugly harassment my sister experienced—threatening letters and emails, spying photographers in front of the house, made-up stories about her family—was a tiny microcosm of what was also happening on the national stage. Long before she received her first threatening missive, many other wildlife gardeners had been slapped down in communities across the country. The mosses that blanket bird nests and soften the hard edges of the world? Banned. The fallen pine cones that provide shelter and food for ladybugs and squirrels? Banned. The rich leafy layer that enriches the soil, shelters butterfly and moth larvae, keeps queen bumblebees warm in winter, and offers a foraging table for countless birds who kick up the seeds and insects underneath? Unequivocally banned and sucked up by giant vacuuming trucks like trash.

For the sake of a fake aesthetic—a collective conformity manufactured in the minds of corporate lawn and pesticide marketers—our culture has sacrificed birds and their soulful songs, bees and the fruits of their buzzing labors, milkweeds and their heady perfumes, and rocks and branches and leaves and all the frogs, salamanders, beetles, and other hidden treasures underneath. We've given up the scentscape, the soundscape, the tastescape, and the touchscape in the name of an arbitrary sightscape that's dead boring at best and most often just plain deadening. In the dominant paradigm, there is virtually

Built in an old flowerpot, this wren nest is made of natural materials that many homeowners associations ban from residential landscapes for the sake of arbitrary aesthetics.

no sightscape at all, nothing for people to look at and no place for animals to hide and perch and take in the view. There is no color but uniform green, subsuming the splash and the flash that butterflies, fireflies, birds, bees, wasps, and so many other animals bring to a more natural garden. A homogenized landscape is a mostly lifeless one, devoid of diversity of colors and visual textures and branching lines that animals actively seek when foraging and nesting.

Raised in a culture of excessive control of outdoor spaces and anesthetized to the losses, we may at first look askance at natural landscapes: the winter browns and faded yellows of toppled grasses and crunching leaves, the summer thickets of shrubs and vines left to grow toward the sun however they wish. But look again, from the eyes of a wren, and what do we see instead? Our own eyes tell us only a small fraction of the story unless we choose to imagine more. Without the courage to think and feel for ourselves, we wait for others to tell us what's beautiful, losing faith in our senses and falling into a pattern of reducing the world to straight lines, artificial palettes, and narrow, predictable expectations.

A picture is only a snapshot of one moment with few layers. It doesn't really tell a thousand words, yet we put all our faith and hopes in single images, as a culture obsessed with how animals and plants look to us rather than how they're looking at the world and what they're smelling, hearing, tasting, and touching. Caught in the crossfire of our contradictory attitudes are living beings with few safe harbors. On private property, we treat wildlife as intruders, alerting police when coyotes wander the neighborhood. On public lands, we ourselves are the intruders, taking selfies with giant turtles and cuddling up to buffaloes. On the surface, the two types of behaviors appear dissimilar—one results from misguided fears and the other from seemingly no fears at all. But they derive from the same view of wild animals as abstractions, a collection of anonymous creatures who are alternately "pests," "nuisances," or subjects for perfect vacation pictures.

During my own travels, I've seen these reductionist sightlines play out on coastlines. In California, where sea lions rest atop the rocks, a mother with young children steps as close as she can with her selfie stick, disturbing a wild mother and her young; a man walks up

A yellow rope encourages vacationers to keep their distance from endangered monk seals in Hawaii. Animals are often seen as either intruders or photo ops.

to touch a sea lion lying near the incoming tide and is startled away when the animal roars up and barks at him. In Hawaii, endangered monk seals are also vulnerable to harassment, protected only by the temporary stringlines that volunteers set up each day around the sleeping families.

Our eyes deceive us more than any other sense, and we misinterpret animals' visual signals. Several years ago, a viral video showed a woman petting two lime-green spicebush swallowtail caterpillars in her hand and cooing affectionately, "When you find things like this, you don't want to play with anything else." Thousands of commenters noted how adorable it was and extolled the wonders of nature, without stopping to consider what it was like to be a tiny animal in the palm of a giant predator. Toward the end of the video, one of the caterpillars started regurgitating, a defense mechanism that no one seemed to notice.

To our eyes, spicebush swallowtail caterpillars, with their huge fake eyespots, look like cute cartoon characters. But their visual trickery is meant to fool birds into thinking they're snakes or perhaps tree frogs. They didn't evolve to scare humans away, but they also didn't evolve to undergo heavy petting. In addition to his findings that caterpillars are stressed by passing traffic, University of Georgia research scientist Andy Davis found that monarch larvae experience a 20 percent increase in heart rate after being gently handled, indicating a fight-or-flight response similar to our own reactions to stress.

Of course, caterpillars can't flee from handsy humans or pesticide-spraying neighbors. As more mobile beings, people ostensibly have more choices in the places they inhabit. Under extreme duress themselves, my sister's family could have taken flight, selling their house and moving away. But giving up on the flowers and wrens and doves and raccoons and butterflies they loved wasn't an option. So they chose to fight. In the end, the HOA floated many untenable alternatives, including a proposed fence, a kind of border wall where no humans or animals could cross, dredging up deep-seated attitudes of entitlement and control that dominate decisions about the lands around us and the arbitrary lines we draw: in the sand, in the turf, and sometimes searingly through the homes of our own neighbors, both human and wild.

But like the monk seal rescue crews in Hawaii, Janet built something better: a wall of compassion and protection around the garden, a place where the Carolina wrens can nest in peace. This expanded sightscape blends human design with a natural aesthetic attractive to people and animals alike: the edges are filled with flowers, not fences, and sedges where butterflies and moths can lay their eggs. Pots of pink and purple annuals flank the entrance, and a large patch of scarlet bee balm lines the front path, waiting to welcome returning hummingbirds, whose own vision stretches the figments—and the very pigments—of our imagination.

Beyond the Rainbow:
Sensory Explosions of a Hummingbird

For a brief moment, he commands the sky. He's not pure flash, and he's not doing just any old song and dance. This guy brings it all—color, swagger, musical interludes—in bedazzling acrobatic displays intended for a female who's ready to scrutinize every groovy move.

That female isn't me, though I'm mesmerized enough. Somewhere in the surrounding trees, a hummingbird mother-to-be is building a nest and looking for just the right mate to father her children. Back and forth her suitor goes, in feather-buzzing, U-shaped dives, starting near the sassafras grove, swooping over the path and pond, rising up fifteen feet next to the tulip trees, and then doing it all in reverse. As soon as the object of his affections perches for a better view of the show, the acrobatic male will draw much closer, performing short, fast

Male broad-tailed hummingbirds have spectacular courtship rituals, creating a sensory explosion of movement, color, and sound.

Our pond has been the scene of dramatic U-shaped dives of ruby-throats.

"shuttle displays" and showing off his gorgeous gorget, the patch of bright red feathers on his throat.

As spectacular as the ruby-throated hummingbird's flirtations are, males of some other species have even more dramatic courtship rituals. Broad-tailed hummingbirds, a western species, fly up to a hundred feet in the air and hover, listening for the chirps of a female indicating, "I see you; I'm interested; show me what you got," says Mary (Cassie) Stoddard, an associate professor of ecology and evolutionary biology at Princeton University. The male then launches a rapid, U-shaped dive, sometimes skillfully coming within inches of a female's head.

Growing up on the East Coast, Stoddard was familiar with the dives of ruby-throated hummingbirds. But that didn't prepare her for the grand shows of the broad-taileds she saw upon arrival at the Rocky Mountain Biological Lab in Colorado, where she was planning experiments on bird color vision. "I'd never seen anything like it in my life," she says, "and I was so amazed that I just thought, 'We have to study that.'"

During dives, the hummingbird's wing feathers vibrate in the wind to produce a cricket-like trill, but at a critical point, the bird spreads his tail feathers to add a different sound. Using video and audio recordings, Stoddard and postdoctoral researcher Ben Hogan pinpointed precise moments when the males create that buzz. A UV-sensitive camera helped them photograph museum specimens at different angles to create a bird's-eye view of how females see males' magenta gorgets throughout their dives. Results showed that broad-tailed hummingbirds coordinate an exquisitely synchronized "sensory explosion" at the base of the dive, says Stoddard.

"What we found is that all the action is happening in a three-hundred-millisecond window, and if you blink your eyes slowly, that's it—about a third of a second. It's pretty fast. The male is reaching his top horizontal speed, he is making a buzz with his tail feathers, and the color change will be the most dramatic during this period, as the perceived color shifts from red to black."

The researchers have proposed several reasons for the burst of color and sound. The birds might be putting all their cards on the table at once so females can judge their skill and fitness. They could be striving for efficiency, taking the quickest path to impressing potential mates. The simultaneous sensory signals might provide backup in case of interference, or the males could simply be indulging a "taste for the beautiful," playing to females' aesthetic preferences. Whatever the case, the findings point to the value of a more holistic approach to research on animals' sensory experiences. "There's increasing recognition that the way we tend to study signals, particularly visual signals, is as if animals are static, lacking the motion and dynamism that is infused in all of these displays," says Stoddard. "And that's because once you add in motion, you have all these spatial and temporal dynamics that are difficult to quantify. But our soapbox message is, 'Well, real animals move—so we must account for this when studying their signals.'"

The hummingbirds led me to Stoddard's work after one took to circling my head for minutes at a time during the first summer of social isolation in 2020, when humans weren't allowed to get close to one another but animals became increasingly bold. Flattered by the attention, and daydreaming that the bird and I possessed a magical connection, I finally realized what was attracting him: my falling-apart glasses, held together at the joint by a sturdy wad of bright red duct tape. It was a DIY fix I'd flaunted all season, waiting for the day I could safely go to a doctor's office again.

Here was the one creature in the world who actually liked my pandemic style, and I regretted misleading him into thinking I might be a flower. But he found nectar in plenty of other places around our habitat, and as I watched him go about his busy days, I realized that many of his watering holes weren't red at all. In between pit stops at his favorite red cardinal flowers and coral honeysuckles, he also went for the white penstemon, the pink thistle and phlox, the purple wild bergamot and ironweed, the blue salvias, the great blue lobelia, and the yellow cup plant.

If they're not as discriminating as we think, I wondered, why have the birding and gardening worlds been so fixated on providing hummingbirds with red flowers? Certainly the boldness of red might be a lure, says Stoddard, and human influence—in the form of massive numbers of red-colored feeders along hummingbirds' migratory routes—likely reinforces a connection between the color and the reward. But beyond that, the color red probably won't make one food source inherently more attractive than another. "Hummingbirds really do have color preferences, there's no doubt about it," says Stoddard. "These preferences are real. But the preferences are not innate. They are learned, and they can be rewired based on new, rewarding conditions. I think hummingbirds can learn these things in a matter of days."

Stoddard saw with her own eyes how quickly hummingbirds learn to associate food with other colors, proving through her experiments that they can make fine-grained decisions between colors that look exactly the same to humans—green and UV-green, for example—to accurately select whichever one is associated with a sweet payoff. Birds, fish, and many reptiles can see what we can't because they're tetrachromatic, meaning they have a fourth color "cone type," or cone-shaped cells in their retinas that are thought to be sensitive to ultraviolet light. The other three types—short-wave, blue-sensing cones; medium-wave, green-sensing cones; and long-wave, red-sensing cones—are similar to those found in the eyes of trichromatic humans.

Many of the colors we see are created when a wavelength of light stimulates two adjacent cones; for example, our eyes perceive yellow when green and red cones are stimulated simultaneously. These colors are considered "spectral" because they appear in the spectrum visible to human eyes, ordered as in a rainbow or light filtered through a prism: deep blue, blue, green, yellow, orange, red. But there are also nonspectral colors—those that aren't in the rainbow and stimulate cones that are widely separated in the visible spectrum of light. We humans perceive only one: purple, which results from the mixing of signals from red and blue cones. The palette of such nonspectral colors available to animals with UV-sensitive cone cells is much broader and includes UV-green, UV-red, and purple, and all the nuanced tones in between.

To learn just how well hummingbirds discern differences between spectral colors and those mixed with ultraviolet, Stoddard's team placed clear dishes atop two tripods with adjustable LED light tubes attached, filling one dish with sugar water and the other with water. A different LED color was displayed at each feeding station. The researchers eliminated the possibility that the birds could rely on

Flowers for hummingbirds don't have
to be red; yellow Carolina jessamine
vine and purple vervain are among
the many plants they enjoy.

spatial cues by swapping the positions of the feeding stations every fifteen minutes. To ensure the birds weren't using scent or following one another to the rewarding feeder, they conducted a control experiment using the same colors for both sugar water and plain water. Under those conditions, "we should expect the birds to just fifty-fifty guess; they don't know where to go," says Stoddard. "And that's exactly what happened."

But when the colors were even slightly varied—for example, two greens combined with different amounts of UV—the birds could tell them apart, learning within hours to go to whichever feeder held the sweet treat. Stoddard knew intellectually that birds can detect ultraviolet, in the same way that she knows the moon and the sun can line up, but witnessing animals perceiving colors outside our visual spectrum was as thrilling as watching a solar eclipse. "I'll never forget it," she says, "and it was really exciting to watch these wild birds perceive something that I couldn't see even though I was standing right next to them."

Examining the plumage of nearly a thousand bird species and the colors of more than two thousand plant species, Stoddard's team found that hummingbirds likely see a third or more of these plumage and plant colors as nonspectral—far more than we humans do. Our color vision is so impoverished in comparison that it's hard to even conceive of what a bird's world must look like, but Stoddard and her colleagues invoked the experience of hearing rich musical layers to consider the possibilities. "Does UV+green appear to birds as a mix of those colors (analogous to a double-stop chord played by a violinist) or as a sublime new color (analogous to a completely new tone unlike its components)?" they asked in their paper. "We cannot say.... Ultimately, what matters to a bird is probably not whether colorful signals are detected by adjacent or nonadjacent cone types: It is how those colors function to provide information about food, mates, or predators."

If hummingbirds don't inherently have an overarching passion for one pigment over another, why do so many flowers that rely on them for pollination—at least 84 percent—come in red? The answer seems to lie not so much in what birds prefer but in which animals the plants would like to deter from visiting their flowers. Many blooms have evolved to fit the bills of their favorite pollinators perfectly; one striking example is the relationship between the passionflower and the sword-billed hummingbird, whose beak is longer than her body, enabling her to reach deep into the long corollas. Adding the color red to the mix might be a way to further reserve nectar for the birds while shooing away less efficient bees, who find red more difficult to detect.

Like humans, bees are trichromatic, but their photoreceptors are sensitive to blue, green, and ultraviolet. That makes them particularly good at locating "nectar guides," a UV-reflecting region found in the center of many flowers. These markings, invisible to us, help bees find food quickly; one study even found that the visual navigational signals also benefit plants by reducing nectar robbery, which occurs when bees steal floral resources through holes in stems without pollinating in return.

But without red-sensing photoreceptors, bees have a hard time seeing red flowers, especially against a background of green foliage. This appears to be the way many hummingbird-pollinated plants prefer it. Through studies of bee and hummingbird plant visitation, scientists have found evidence to support "the bee-avoidance hypothesis": bees often pollinate flowers on the same individual plants more frequently, a behavior that can lead to lower seed set. By making themselves less discernible to bees, plants can save precious resources for hummingbirds, increase their chances of cross-pollination, and encourage genetic diversity among their populations.

How the hummingbirds really see flowers, we'll never quite know. Early vertebrates had four color cone types, and many animals retained this way of seeing the world. But mammals were small, nocturnal creatures who lived underground and didn't require such a rich visual experience. They lost two of the cone types, and most mammals are still dichromatic, says Stoddard. "It wasn't until dinosaurs died out that mammals really diversified into new niches and habitats. Eventually, the Old World primates duplicated one of the two remaining color cone types in mammals to create the third color cone type that we humans enjoy today. A lot of people ask, 'Why is UV special for birds? Why did they get it and not us?' But the fact is, birds didn't gain it; our mammal ancestors lost it."

Yet even with our more deprived color palette, the world is still a rainbow of possibilities, sometimes emanating from the most unlikely places.

Prettiest in Pink: A Glam Planthopper

Pink is an ancient home carved into a sandstone cliff in the desert, and it's a roseate spoonbill feasting on shrimp and crayfish in the tidal marsh. Pink is the long dress with the puffy sleeves that my mom

Most planthoppers are as green as a leaf, with veining to match, but this glam girl in my habitat looked more like a cherry blossom petal.

made for my sister's prom, and it's the short one covered in blue bumblebees that we both wore to nursery school. Pink was my grandpa, a boilermaker and cinnamon bun baker whose tough skin matched the roses my grandma grew, and pink was the polish on our nails when he teased us for having "pearly toes." Pink is the peonies that bloomed in my dad's garden the week after he died, and it's the scar on my mom's fragile arm that reopens when she bumps into things. Pink is the swamp milkweed flower in Janet's garden that draws all the monarchs in the neighborhood. Pink is beauty and sunrise and wounds and sunset.

Pink is a lot of things, but pink is not supposed to be the planthopper. Planthoppers are the color of spring leaves, with intricate veining to match. Like katydids, they're so well blended into their surroundings that they've eluded me all these years, until one afternoon when I spot a tiny pink speck on a viburnum leaf. From six feet away, it looks like a fallen cherry blossom petal. But it's mid-August, and there are no pink-flowering trees or shrubs in bloom.

Walking slowly toward the mystery critter, I get close enough to see the beautiful rounded shape of an insect with violet eyes. No one will believe this without proof, so I snap a few shots, and in my eagerness to get to know her better, I move too close. Poof! The seven-millimeter glam girl is gone in a flash, living up to her name and leaping away.

I've arbitrarily decided she's female. I'll never know for sure, but identifying the species of my fleeting friend is easier, thanks to the pretty markings that edge her wings: she's a two-striped planthopper, *Acanalonia bivittata*. Despite their passing resemblance to katydids and grasshoppers in the order Orthoptera, planthoppers are "true bugs," in the order Hemiptera. As sap-sucking insects who lay eggs in the stems of many different species, the two-striped planthoppers' diet is so wide ranging that they leave little trace, leading insect authorities to conclude they're "economically unimportant" because they don't bother our food crops.

The pink planthopper is important to me, though, and I want to learn everything I can about why she stands out from the crowd. This proves trickier, since research is scant and appears to be confined mostly to taxonomy and, in the case of planthopper species considered "pests," agricultural studies. If I wanted to know more about the accidentally introduced spotted lanternfly, an Asian planthopper whose presence has caused no end of alarmist behavior—including encouraging impressionable children to kill them—I could find plenty of information and people willing to speak with me. I could even don hats and pins and put stickers on my car that incite people to commit violence against the insect by stomping on them.

No such attention is heaped upon two-striped planthoppers, though their interesting behavior at the nymphal stage has been the subject of speculation. Producing waxy filaments from glands in their abdomens, the nymphs look like tiny conch shells with a spray of fuzzy tail emanating from their backsides. Theories about the function of planthopper wax range from preventing desiccation to enabling nymphs to float if they fall into puddles to heading off their capture in spiderwebs. Planthoppers secrete honeydew as they eat, so the waxy bits may also keep them from getting stuck in their own goo. Many planthopper species produce waxes at different life stages, noted the authors of a 2014 review for the American Entomological Society, "but the biological functions and taxonomic distribution of wax production remains poorly investigated."

Breeding experiments have shown that pink is likely a dominant color in katydids, and green is recessive, despite the rare occurrence of the more conspicuous coloration.

Until a few years ago, it wasn't even clear how planthoppers communicated: an overlooked vibratory part on the abdomen, which the authors of a 2019 paper dubbed "the snapping organ," uses a fast elastic recoil to send signal pulses through the planthoppers' legs to the substrates they're perched on. It's a big world out there for a tiny animal, and such mechanisms help them send love letters with a broad range of frequencies to potential mates.

With so little known about their basic biology, it's not a surprise to find a dearth of information about my planthopper's unusual coloration. It's a relatively uncommon phenomenon; a passage in the 1932 *Annals of the Entomological Society of America* noted that in a collection of four hundred planthoppers, only seven were pink or red. More celebrated than planthoppers, pink katydids are said to be a one-in-five-hundred occurrence, making headlines when they're discovered in backyards and parks from Ontario to Illinois to Pennsylvania. In New Zealand, a Wellington man trimming hedges was just as fooled by the pinkness as I was: "Initially I thought it was just a pink petal that had fallen off," he told the *Dominion Post*. "But then I realized it was moving."

Katydids are also slightly more studied. For many years scientists believed that the pink ones resulted from a genetic mutation controlled by recessive genes that lead to excessive amounts of carotenoids—which give carrots their color—or by reduction of other pigments. Sometimes referred to as erythrism, unusual pinkness has also been observed in manta rays, leopards, badgers, and other insects such as grasshoppers.

But about fifteen years ago, entomologists at the Audubon Butterfly Garden and Insectarium in New Orleans added a new twist to the story. After breeding katydids of multiple colors in a series of experiments, the researchers came to a surprising conclusion: pink and yellow appear to be dominant traits in oblong-winged katydids, while green is likely recessive.

A donation of eight wild-caught male and female pink katydids had kicked off the quest to learn more about the inheritance of coloration in 2008, and another donation of wild yellow and orange katydids enhanced the experiments. To test the long-held theory that the bright colors were a result of mutations controlled by recessive genes, the team encouraged mating of differently colored pairs: pink females with pink males, pink females with green males, pink males with green females, yellow males with yellow females, green males with green females, and a free-for-all "rainbow cage" of yellow, orange, and pink males and females.

Under the rules of genetic inheritance developed by Gregor Mendel, color morphs result from different combinations of alleles, or variants of a gene that sit in the same spot on a pair of chromosomes. Organisms with two different types of alleles are heterozygous, with one allele expressing a dominant color and one a recessive color. Dominant alleles mask recessive ones, so only those that are homozygous, receiving two recessive alleles from their parents, would possess the rarer pigmentation. In humans, we're familiar with this concept when we think of blue eyes and blond hair, which are made possible by the joining of recessive genes and the absence of the dominant color brown.

If pink were a recessive color in katydids, two pink parents' combined recessive genes would make green offspring impossible. But instead, the researchers in Louisiana found that 11 percent of the katydids born to pink parents were green, indicating that the pink parents possessed a pink and green allele and that pink was far more dominant. Conversely, mating of green males and green females who'd come from pink parents yielded no pink offspring—a uniformity that could not have happened unless green were a recessive trait. "In neither of those crosses did any pink emerge," wrote entomologist Jayme Necaise and his colleague Tabitha Holloway. "This strongly suggests that the predominant genotype in nature is homozygous recessive green."

If pink is dominant in katydids—and assuming the same might be true for planthoppers—why are there so few of these insects? And how could they persist if their color makes them so easily spotted by predators? When I asked Louisiana entomologist Gary Noel Ross, who once studied a pink katydid he found in a prairie, he answered my questions with more questions: "When those pink katydids and pink planthoppers began appearing, who knows what the ecosystems were like back then? Because it wasn't yesterday that this happened. It probably didn't even begin in our geologic era. This may go back to the Mesozoic. Who knows what was going on then? We're looking at things today in a short time span and forgetting that these things evolved millions of years ago when the world was very different, the atmosphere was very different, the plant life was different." Maybe, Ross notes, there were more pink plants to blend into.

In the early 2000s, Ross gleaned some clues while surveying butterflies in the Wah'Kon-Tah Prairie in Missouri. Sitting in a patch of pale purple coneflower to wait for regal fritillaries to flutter by, he saw someone else instead. "I noticed this pinky on the coneflower, and I thought, wow, what a beautiful adaptation!" He brought the katydid home with him, placed her in a terrarium, and gave her native grasses and leaves from the prairie to eat. But the katydid wasn't having any of it. Worried she'd die, Ross recalled the plant he had found her on and brought her a coneflower bloom. She immediately began nibbling. "Pink flowers are certainly a standout on the prairie; they're one of the most beautiful flowers there," says Ross, "and I would imagine there are quite a few insects and maybe other things that have adapted to those colors in order to escape predation."

Wondering if the katydid would change color based on her diet, he also brought her yellow blooms. "But even though she feasted on yellow for the rest of her two-month confinement, I found no hint of jaundice," Ross wrote in a 2003 article in *Natural History* magazine. "Apparently it was in her nature, not her nurture."

Though the katydid never did eat the greens Ross offered, Necaise found that the colonies he raised in the lab had voracious appetites, eating many native plants and also lettuce, sweet potatoes, oranges, zucchini, and even Cheerios. "At first, I too thought the pink individuals may find protection on pink flowers and want to behaviorally adapt to resting on those color plants for the camouflage protection it may afford them," Necaise responded when I wrote to him about my planthopper mystery. "However, after hours of observation with a choice of plants to rest on, the pink individuals were not more likely to hang out on a pink flower than they were a green leaf."

Still, I had to wonder whether in the wilder environment of my backyard, my planthopper knew she was sitting on something that didn't properly accessorize with her outfit? Looking more closely again at the area where I first spotted the planthopper, I saw that the stems of the viburnum she perched on were indeed pink, as were newly emerging leaves. Not only that, but the garden was filled all summer with a succession of pink and lavender flowers—phlox, hibiscus, joe-pye, wild bergamot, purple coneflower, horse nettle, swamp milkweed, common milkweed, and native thistles—and the latter two are both known to host planthoppers.

Maybe the persistence of the pink planthoppers helps enlarge the species' niche by enabling some individuals to match and feed on a broader diversity of flowers. "There is definitely some evolutionary advantage to that," Ross speculates, "an evolutionary advantage that is allowing it to survive where others wouldn't." Or maybe, as Necaise suggests, the seemingly incongruous abundance of a recessive green coloration is a result of "directional selection," which occurs when one allele leads to greater fitness and becomes more frequent regardless of its genetic dominance or lack thereof. "Pink colored individuals would certainly be very conspicuous to predators," he wrote in the katydid paper. "Because they are pink during molting and development, it is suggested that many of these colored individuals would be preyed upon well before they reach adulthood or shortly thereafter. The small percentage of pink individuals in wild populations that do achieve sexual maturity and do breed with green produce approximately 50 percent pink and 50 percent green. This could explain why the pink coloration is so rare in nature, but not completely eradicated."

Though pink katydids were born pink in Necaise's studies, yellow and orange ones didn't show their true colors until the last stage of metamorphosis, when they became wildly conspicuous, with some parading orange bodies and green eyes or yellow bodies on pink legs. "This puts these yellow and orange colored individuals at a selective advantage over pinks during the early stages of life," he noted. "They are green, so they have camouflage."

In Madagascar, planthoppers known as *Phromnia rosea* blend in by being bold, gathering their bright pink bodies together along stems to create the impression of a flower spike, a kind of synchronized dance of deception to predators. Who's to say ours didn't once do that here too?

We only knew each other for a flashing moment, but the colorful character in my garden with the Liz Taylor eyes has taught me much more than I ever expected to learn about her kind. Pink *is* the planthopper, and why that's so remains a marvelous mystery.

Trogus species have no common name, so I call this one the eclipse wasp—a nod to her coloration and her appearance on a day when the sun and the moon briefly aligned.

Trogus wasps might have evolved their coloration to look as scary as rusty spider wasps like this one. Spider wasps can more easily fight back against predators, using the same powerful stingers they deploy on their prey.

Costume Parties

When her iridescent blue wings close, she is twilight. When they open, she is fiery dawn. All around her, the light is receding, turning summer's primary colors to pastels. But from her perch on a rhododendron leaf, this spectacular being shows no signs of being muted. She has a full afternoon's work ahead of her, and no time for otherworldly events.

We're alone in the quieting universe. Will is five hundred miles south of here, standing in an open field to watch the moon dance with the sun. The view of the solar eclipse in Maryland isn't expected to be so grand, but, like the wasp, I have other things to do, so I've stayed home.

Just a few steps out the back door and a few feet from the ground, though, the scenery is as magnificent as anything I could have spied in the sky. Walking among the crescent-shaped moon shadows filtering through the spicebushes and sassafras trees onto the patio, I didn't expect to meet anyone new today, especially not someone who's considered relatively hard to find. It will be years, if ever, before I see her kind again. But her timing is as brilliant as her color palette.

Known scientifically as *Trogus pennator* or *Trogus vulpinus*—the two species are so closely related that I would have had to examine her more thoroughly to say definitively—the wasp has no common name. Her Latin-and-Greek-derived names roughly translate to "gnawing feather" or "gnawing fox," not the prettiest ways to describe such a perfect host for a celestial event. To me, she is the eclipse wasp, a creature who can turn light into darkness and back again with the flip of a wing.

Harmless to us, the eclipse wasp has an unusual nesting site: the caterpillars of swallowtail butterflies. She injects a single egg into each caterpillar she finds; when the wasp egg hatches, the larva feeds on and eventually kills the developing host. Instead of a new adult butterfly exiting a swallowtail chrysalis, a wasp emerges. Though the gutting of butterfly babies may sound gruesome, it helps to remember how important these parasitoids are to plants—and that birds also devour caterpillars, but we don't hold birds' predatory ways against them.

Because of her location, I can only assume that our eclipse wasp's swallowtail caterpillar of choice is the spicebush swallowtail, who eats the leaves of spicebushes and sassafras trees. Slow-moving and often hiding in rolled-up leaves, these cartoonish creatures may be vulnerable to misguided humans showing off for social media, but they aren't completely defenseless against other animals. They take a two-stage approach to visual disguise, with the early-stage larvae looking like brown and white bird droppings, blending into the scenery. It's only later that they shed the scatological look for the more people-pleasing green color and huge eyespots. But while their color patterns might fend off birds, they're no match for the wasps, who rely on swallowtails exclusively for reproduction.

To find these living egg-laying sites, the wasps follow their eyes and antennae. In entomologist Karen Sime's study of *Trogus pennator* wasps and caterpillars of zebra swallowtail butterflies in Florida, the wasps appeared to use visual cues to locate pawpaw trees, the butterflies' host plants, from a distance. But, as her later research showed, the wasps were probably also following the scent of the plants. Once close enough, they could distinguish between the odors of plants nibbled by caterpillars and those that were still intact. Upon landing,

An emerald moth caterpillar pretends she's a flower by dressing herself in petals of purple coneflower.

An emerald moth caterpillar masquerades as a brown-eyed Susan.

they used their antennae to search for frass and evidence of feeding. Swallowtail larvae have an interesting defense mechanism, extending a forked, brightly colored organ coated with strong-smelling chemicals to repel ants and spiders, but the weaponry doesn't always deter *Trogus pennator*. If they're lucky, though, their mothers have already deployed another evasion tactic by depositing eggs on young, short pawpaws protected by fallen leaves, laying low enough to escape the notice of the high-flying, dashing eclipse wasps.

The wasps themselves are also trying to avoid predation. But rather than hiding, they stand out in screaming color, nature's way of warning others they'll be sorry. When an animal's bold colors and patterns are accompanied by strong chemicals or other defense mechanisms—think of the orange and black of the monarch or the contrasting stripes of a skunk—she's considered aposematic. When the colors are a bluff, though, she's simply a mimic. Spicebush swallowtail adults tell these visual fibs through their resemblance to their well-defended cousins, the pipevine swallowtails, who sequester aristolochic acids from their host plants. Many such lookalikes are all talk and no toxin, but they gain protections by association.

False advertising appears to be the primary defense of my eclipse wasp friend too. *Trogus* species are members of Ichneumonidae, a family of wasps who have ovipositors, or egg-laying tubes, rather than painful stingers. While they can harm other insects by laying their eggs in them, they can't deploy a strong defensive weapon against would-be attackers. Their flashy appearance might be an imitation of someone more able to fight back, possibly rusty spider wasps, who are well-equipped with stingers to paralyze spiders for their nests.

Pretty pretenders in the garden come in many other surprising forms. Some caterpillars in the *Synchlora* genus live the life I've always dreamed of, surrounded by and covered in flowers. Liatris, purple coneflowers, and brown-eyed Susans are some of their favorites—so much so that the caterpillars cut off pieces of the petals and other plant parts and attach them to their bodies. Sharp-eyed gardeners might spot the slow movements of these wildly beautiful creatures who look ready to join Carnival.

Our home in Maryland falls in the overlapping range of two of these fabulous costume-partygoers: the wavy-lined emerald moth (*Synchlora aerata*) and the Southern emerald moth (*Synchlora frondaria).* Caterpillars of both species are excellent practitioners of crypsis, the term for making yourself invisible through visual or other sensory signals. On their own, they would stick out like a toucan in a corporate boardroom, but against a floral backdrop they become wallflowers, melting into their surroundings. In a 1979 study of wavy-lined emerald moths, researchers watched the caterpillars change their outfits based on the venue, carefully cutting flower parts with their mandibles, adding a mucilaginous substance to them, and attaching them to specialized hooks on their backs. When moved back and forth between purple liatris and yellow goldenrods, the caterpillars even switched up their sewing patterns. Donning a liatris costume involved cutting fragments of petals, but creating a substantial camouflage out of small-flowered goldenrod meant cutting and attaching entire flowerheads.

Regular maintenance keeps their stylish looks in pristine condition, something I notice one morning after seeing a caterpillar on brown-eyed Susans with wilted brown petals still attached to her back from the day before. Three hours later, she's dressed to the nines again, in full yellow and orange regalia. Heading out back to spy on her cousin on the coneflower, I notice something else interesting: beneath this caterpillar's petal streamers, her body looks as purple as the flower itself. A study of Southern emerald moths from 2009 offers a possible explanation, documenting the species' propensity not only to dress up in flowers but to actually change its larval color to match—a disguise the researchers called the "double cloak of invisibility."

Such behavioral and visual flexibility offers an obvious advantage to the caterpillars, helping them dine unseen on a wide range of plants. If, like monarch or spicebush swallowtail caterpillars, they had

Crab spiders can change color to match flowers, helping the spiders to catch unsuspecting prey.

been born with a preprogrammed set of permanent colors and food preferences, then they would be stuck with a limited palette. But the ability of these generalist herbivores to blend into a broader range of colors and textures probably has something to do with their spread across the South, the Caribbean, and Central and South America.

Flower imposters aren't just confined to camouflaging caterpillars; other organisms take on floral decor to lure prey or enlist help in propagation. On Orchid Island in the Luzon Strait, near the Philippines, researchers found that the bright yellow markings on an orb-weaving spider were critical to attracting insects, who apparently mistake the patterns and contrasts for flower petals or pollen. Fungi engage in such fakery too; USDA researchers have documented a *Fusarium* species that hijacks two perennial grass species in the *Xyris* genus in Guyana, creating "pseudoflowers" that imitate the grasses' real yellow blooms and even produce floral volatiles. The goal, of course, is to attract bees who will then spread spores and help the fungi reproduce.

Humans hold grand celebrations of our thespian talents, but other organisms were great actors long before we ever came onto the scene. The most ancient known efforts by insects are immortalized in Spanish, Burmese, French, and Lebanese amber. Examination of fossils more than a hundred million years old reveals unique debris-carrying structures in lacewing larvae and assassin bugs; their chosen costume accessories included sand grains, dust, leaf trichomes (or hairs), wood fibers, bits of ferns, and the exoskeletons of insects they likely preyed upon.

That may sound like the grotesque behavior of human trophy hunters who proudly display their shameless and unnecessary kills, but the insects' motivation is purely survival. Larvae of modern green lacewing species also make use of leaves, spider thread, and other materials in their environment; some even don waxy filaments pulled off the bodies of woolly aphids they've consumed. In the absence of this clever disguise, ants who farm and protect aphids for their honeydew secretions will go on the attack against the lacewings for just trying to snag a meal. And if you ever see a lichen on legs ambling around a tree trunk, that's a lacewing larva hiding her identity while foraging. Some people call them "trash bugs," but these beautiful and inventive animals are fashionistas.

Plants wear visual disguises too, and not just to attract pollinators. Sometimes they need to turn away the overeager types, and what better way to do that than to post a "No Vacancy" sign? Some posers change their own morphology to fool herbivores like caterpillars who could otherwise swallow them whole. In the tropical Americas, female butterflies in the *Heliconius* genus lay eggs on passionflower vines, but they judiciously avoid spots where other butterflies have already

Gray tree frogs are true to their name when hiding between bricks, but they turn green to blend in with plants.

Lacewing larvae often attach lichen to their backs to disguise themselves from predators. Some get even more creative, adding bits and bobs of plant and animal matter.

done so. It's a wise move, as the larvae of many *Heliconius* species eat eggs and other larvae. The voraciousness of these butterfly babies can also present a problem for the vines if they are quickly defoliated. By developing structures that look like the yellow eggs of *Heliconius*, the shapeshifting vines tell their own lies, encouraging hovering butterflies to move along.

Color shifters are among the most talented visual artists. Crab spiders can match the flowers they sit on to avoid detection by unsuspecting prey. Gray tree frogs can blend into their surroundings to make themselves invisible to predators. In spite of their common name, these tiny amphibians can also be green, a trait better indicated by their scientific name, *Hyla versicolor*.

Unlike American toads, who can secrete a mildly poisonous substance called bufotoxin, gray tree frogs lack chemical defenses and depend completely on camouflage. Their ever-changing appearance fools many a predator, including humans; the gray tree frogs sitting on my friend's lilies in Minnesota look bright green—and like a different species from the ones who perch on a gate in my Maryland habitat, becoming almost indistinguishable from the weathered wood. The mottled pattern on their backs enhances the disguise, resembling the lichen on the trees they inhabit. Sometimes these little masters of disguise surprise us by hiding in plain sight, even squeezing themselves between bricks and blending seamlessly into the mortar. The only thing giving them away is their trilling calls as Will walks past. Is he a predator or a competitor—or are the frogs wolf-whistling at my husband?

If they had been really worried about Will's encroachment on their territory, they might have leapt away and flashed the underside of their legs, revealing a startling orange-yellow intended to confuse predators. These bright colors also come in handy when the frogs are wee ones and haven't yet left the pond. At the larval stage, many amphibians flexibly change their behavior, appearance, or morphology in the presence of predators. Instead of blending in as they do later in life, gray tree frog tadpoles make their behinds flashy. "They get these chemical cues of predation, which for the most part seems to be when they smell the smell of other members of their species being eaten—like chewed-up tadpole parts in the water," says Eastern Kentucky University's Cy Mott. "Something kicks in, and their tails get to be this bright red or bright orange color, and that's meant as a diversion." Even if the predator eats the tip, it's expendable, so the tadpole can swim along.

Dazzling colors help some reptiles defend themselves too. Young five-linked skinks, brilliantly beautiful lizards who've nested in the logs of our front garden, don't even wait for their sapphire-blue tails to be eaten. They can just drop their twitching appendages altogether, leaving them to thrash about and distract predators while the skinks dash for cover under rocks or logs. The tails grow back—and the skinks find more good uses for them at the adult stage, when males wrap their tails around females while mating and females coil them around eggs while nesting.

For animals and plants, blending in and standing out in the landscape is a matter of survival. For humans, it's a choice, and many people choose to blend into blandness, wearing the mask of the responsible neighbor who mows his lawn once a week, or the tidy homeowner who leaf-blows and stump-grinds away the understory, or the well-off family who can afford to hire a company to do all of that for them. But far from protecting anyone, our forms of crypsis are pretenses that banish other lives from the premises and impoverish our own in the process. Instead of blending into the barrenscape next door, why not try blending into nature, turning the trees and their leaves and the colorful cast of wild characters they shelter into sparkling centerpieces of the neighborhood?

Making Their Own Light

The light that was snuffed out of my life by my dad's death comes back to me one gentle evening in June, when I sit in a chair outside and see two flash dancers on my knee. The fireflies haven't chosen me as a landing place; I've inadvertently picked them up on my sweatpants as I walk along a garden path near the driveway. Still, even to a person who doesn't follow any particular religion, they seem heaven-sent.

Fireflies tend to inspire such associations, holding a strong place in our collective cultural imaginations. In her book *Fireflies, Glow-Worms, and Lightning Bugs*, Lynn Frierson Faust recounted stories from across the globe connecting fireflies with otherworldly phenomena. They've been the eyes of ghosts in the Peruvian Andes and the spirits of the dead "controlled by an unseen mind" in Borneo. In Japan, where the word *hotaru* means both "firefly" and "harmony," the ethereal insects have been revered for a thousand years, representing love as well as the departed souls of warriors. On this continent, Faust wrote, Navajo people have spoken of First Woman's request to Fireman to create the constellations in the sky, which came

Turfgrass is anathema to fireflies, who need plants to perch on, moist spots to lay their eggs, and a pesticide-free environment.

to represent the small, fire-carrying creatures of the Earth. Apache people traced the origins of fire to wily Fox hiding cedar bark in his tail, lighting it in a bonfire started by fireflies and spreading it to the world.

These iconic insects have their own stories to tell, yet we hardly know them at all. Of the 169 described firefly species in the United States, at least 18 are threatened with extinction. But of those thought to exist in the world, "there's an estimated 20 to 30 percent of new firefly species yet to be discovered," says Ben Pfeiffer, founder of the

Texas-based organization Firefly Conservation and Research. Until the 1990s, researchers didn't even know that species of synchronous fireflies—whose males flash simultaneously in search of females hiding in the fallen leaves—occurred in the United States. Traveling overseas to study them in Southeast Asia, scientists weren't aware of what Faust had known since childhood until she finally persuaded them to check it out for themselves: synchronous fireflies lighting up the forests of the Smoky Mountains in Tennessee every summer.

Since then, tens of thousands of tourists have descended on the area to witness this spectacular light show each year. Though I understand the attraction, the disturbance such crowds can bring is cause for concern. As wild residents of a national park, the fireflies in the Smokies at least enjoy more protections than some of their overseas counterparts. Tourists traveling to Thailand and Malaysia to see synchronous fireflies lighting up trees along mangrove rivers might not realize just how devastating their visits can be. In her book *Silent Sparks*, firefly advocate Sara Lewis, a professor at Tufts University, describes the heartbreaking consequences of unchecked exploitation: new resorts and restaurants displacing firefly habitat and casting bright outdoor lights that disrupt mating rituals; water pollution and riverbank erosion from a growing number of diesel-powered boats; tour guides who crash their boats into trees and dislodge flashing males to show to passengers; and residents who are so fed up with all the noise and traffic that they cut down the trees and leave males without a place to sparkle.

Given the number of firefly species and their broad range—they inhabit every state and province of the United States and Canada except Hawaii—many people don't have to look far to watch them.

Yet each year, a million people around the globe travel to distant places to see fireflies. I can't help but wonder how much better life could be for fireflies (and us) if all that time and money were spent instead on appreciating them and nurturing their habitat in our own backyards and communities. Everyone living within range of nocturnal fireflies should be able to walk outside and still see this incredible phenomenon, and many more people could if they let plants grow again.

Lit from within by the reaction of luciferase enzymes with luciferin and other molecules, the fireflies on my knee flashed back and forth in a language only they could fully decipher. At least two species live here, twinkling across the meadow at dusk and rising high up into the trees like stardust deep into the night. Not all fireflies flash; some day-active species known as "dark fireflies" are thought to use pheromones to locate mates. But larvae of all firefly species carry their own inner lights, and we've even arrived home from late nights out to find them flashing their way across the driveway to get from one rich micro-habitat of fallen leaves to another. Flashing is thought to have first evolved as a way to warn predators away from these firefly babies by indicating the toxins within; fireflies contain lucibufagins, which are cardiac glycosides similar to those secreted by toads and collected by monarchs from milkweed. Only later in their evolutionary history did the flashing signals of danger develop into visual love songs. Adults also light up in times of competition, rejection, annoyance, and danger, but most often the flashing is a kind of sexting, with males typically twinkling while flying and females responding from a stationary perch.

It takes years to learn firefly language, says Pfeiffer, a tech entrepreneur whose journey into the world of fireflies began in 2008 when he heard a brief story on NPR about their declines. He'd happened to buy the domain name "Firefly.org" just a few months before, and the moment seemed so serendipitous that he decided to create a website. After years of fieldwork and intense study to learn the taxonomy, morphology, and distribution of Texas fireflies, Pfeiffer can now walk into many habitats in Texas and "read the landscape, or read all the flashes," he says. It's a bit like deciphering Morse code, identifying species by noting the duration between flashes, the number of pulses, the color, and other aspects relating to rhythm and quality of light.

Though many of us may never pick up on all their communications, we don't need to speak their language to understand the well-documented habitat needs of fireflies. And those needs don't look anything like what can (and can't) be found in the typical North American yard. "The lawnmower is one of the biggest enemies of the firefly," says Pfeiffer, who lives in one of Texas's fastest-growing cities, New Braunfels. As human populations increase, they stunt the growth of the plants that support the insects. "It's just been unbelievable the amount of people who come in, and the first thing they do when they buy land on a river is they decide it needs to be mowed like a park—that everything needs to be mowed down, and you need to put a bench there and plant some turfgrass."

Though fireflies generally don't eat as adults and larvae are carnivorous, plants are critical to them for mating, reproduction, and escape from predators. At night, broad-leaved shrubs and trees provide "operational cover," says Pfeiffer, for adults to hide in and flash from. During the day, tall grasses obscure resting fireflies, later serving as launching pads for night flight.

Diverse canopy layers are important to firefly courtship. As males twinkle out their love songs, females take prime seats in the grasses, leafy ground layers, or shrubs to enjoy the show. Females of many species don't fly, but they still need a good view. "A lot of times I'll find females, oddly enough, in the five-foot range in certain habitats, and so you're like, wow, how did you get so high up there?" Pfeiffer says. "She's really just trying to get as high up as she can to look at as many males as possible, basically, so she chooses the right one."

For eggs and larvae, native plants play a critical role by holding soil in the ground layers, where mother fireflies lay eggs in mud, rotting logs, mosses, and fallen leaves. Pine needles can be another important substrate for egg laying, and the pines themselves can help block disruptive light pollutants like glaring all-night security lights from neighboring yards. A close-cropped lawn with none of these natural elements is no place for firefly babies, who are especially vulnerable to drying out. It also leaves them hungry. "That leaf litter creates a place for snails and slugs and worms to occupy," says Pfeiffer, "and that's what the larvae eat."

Some nonnative plants can also dry the soil, making the environment inhospitable to fireflies. If they're invasive, like the carrizo cane grass that Pfeiffer sees along waterways, they can leave potential mates in the dark. "It's ten feet tall and really dense, just like a wall, so it's not creating any great habitat for fireflies because the female's on the ground, and she's trying to signal to a male at the top, who's ten feet away," he says. "She's not going to see him because there's so much vegetation in the way."

Fireflies are generally homebodies, not prone to packing their bags and moving on. The widespread *Photinus pyralis*, also known as the big dipper firefly because of the J-shaped flashes the male writes across the landscape, is more adaptable than many. But scientists have found low gene flow even among their populations. If less-abundant species are similarly attached to their territories—and from all indications they do appear to have short dispersal distances—that could spell trouble for many of them. The very trait that makes it easy to protect fireflies in little-disturbed habitats can make it even easier to wipe out whole breeding populations until "the candle flame gets snuffed out," as Lewis put it, noting the tenuous existence of a population of *Photinus marginellus* that lives only in a small grove of cherry trees outside Boston. "Remarkably, their entire life cycle from egg to adult and back again to egg appears to be carried out beneath these trees," she wrote. "Luckily for them their habitat sits on conservation land that's protected from development, so they will continue to thrive."

Even if that population disappears, the species is at least present in many other places. The same can't be said for fireflies whose habitats are extremely specialized, like those who make their homes in the sand dunes of the Delaware coast. Only a few years ago, the area around Bethany Beach was so dark that Will and I could walk through the lapping tides at 9 P.M. and see the stars at our feet—bioluminescent dinoflagellates that washed ashore and glowed green where we stepped. Now the many mansions overtaking the sands could wipe out another natural night light: the most imperiled firefly in North America, *Photuris bethaniensis*.

Rediscovered in the late 1990s after staying under the radar for nearly fifty years, *P. bethaniensis* lives only in freshwater swales between oceanside dunes and has been found in seven sites in the state, six of them on public lands. Sea level rise, pesticides, fragmentation, and light pollution are major threats, but destruction of the wetlands is the most imminent danger of all. The site with the greatest number of *P. bethaniensis* is on private property where a luxury housing developer began constructing elevated driveways, inspiring a petition for an emergency listing under the federal Endangered Species Act. In their arguments, scientists from the Xerces Society for Invertebrate Conservation and the Center for Biological Diversity noted the sad irony of the threatened demise of creatures whose kind have survived a hundred million years on Earth. "The lucibufagin toxins protect them from predators," they wrote, "but, unfortunately, cannot protect them from anthropogenic threats."

The Bethany Beach fireflies are being sacrificed for the sake of an ocean view, while farther inland, just a couple of houses away on my rural road, habitat for other firefly species vanished in a flash when a series of house-flipping owners traded shrubs, trees, and wildflower gardens for a mowed-down view of the tiny stream behind them. Misguided actions like these are what make protecting any remaining habitats, no matter how small, even more important. In his nocturnal outings, Pfeiffer has made many discoveries in natural areas, including a rare species in central Texas that hadn't been seen in a hundred years. But much closer to human activity, he finds fireflies flashing away in the most unlikely places, even under an oak tree in a tiny wild patch near a commercial center. "Eighteen wheelers are zooming by, and there's this parking lot that's devoid of any life except for people that are going to the Walmart," he recalls. "So these little habitats can help for sure on some level."

The fireflies who lit a welcome flame into the darkness of my grief seemed content for quite a while with the habitat of my cotton-covered knee, likely communicating in either a courtship dialogue or male-to-male competition. "The third possibility," wrote Faust when I sent her a video clip, "is that one of them was a predatory female *Photuris* trying to lure in an unsuspecting male." False advertising is another talent of some fireflies. Not only do some males "pseudo-flash," imitating females to draw competition away, but females in the *Photuris* genus (not to be confused with *Photinus*) trick males of other species to get what they want. Since they're not as well-equipped with toxins, they acquire them in a rather violent way. By mimicking firefly responses of *Photinus* females, these femme fatales can draw *Photinus* males in closer and, if successful, eat them to collect lucibufagins they later pass on to their eggs.

Fireflies may not always know how to live in peace with one another, but it's well within our power to live more gracefully with them. Old graveyards left relatively undisturbed are an especially good place to go firefly-watching, but it shouldn't take the death of humans to bring back other life forms. Once confined only to our backyard, fireflies now sparkle across the front too, likely because we ditched the mower years ago and began nurturing sea oats and other native grasses, sedges, and wildflowers. And though we've added plants, we've never added light. We encourage the fireflies to bring that instead. At night our windows are covered in light-blocking shades and curtains. Outdoor lights are usually off, and we use the flashlights on our phones to navigate the paths. Fireflies can easily reside among the living, connecting us in spirit with our late fathers and mothers and ancestors who could never have imagined a world without them.

Reflections and Mirages

I was in the womb the first time I heard a bird hit a window. The bird died and my mother cried as I bathed in the warmth of her belly. "The sound was terrible," she recalls, repeating the words I've heard many times over my lifetime. At eighty-five years old, she still cries when she says them.

Of course, I don't remember that first strike. But in my longtime job with an animal welfare organization, I heard the thwacking sound of finality often from inside our corporate glass house. Where birds thought they saw more trees, they saw only reflections, a mirage that masked the cubicles sprouting in place of their former habitat. Appeals to the upper echelons fell flat for too long, until finally measures were taken to mitigate the senseless losses. Upstairs the executive offices received fancier window treatments, but downstairs the building manager applied washable beige paint. We couldn't see out very well, a situation that upset some of my colleagues, but at least the birds were no longer flying into a forest that wasn't there.

The most recent time I heard a bird hit a window, I saw her too. She was a wood thrush, and I'd been watching her from our front room for several minutes as she foraged among the leaves under the chokeberries and then led her mate in a courtship dance. Around they swung in fast, circular flights, swooping low from the chokeberries to the front hedge and back again, only pausing to catch their breath together on the branch of a silver maple. Wood thrushes are shy, reclusive forest birds, and though we hear their ethereal song from early morning until well into the evening, we had never seen this before. I beckoned Will over quietly so he could witness the magical

Wood thrushes swoop low among shrubs during courting and are vulnerable to crashing into reflective windows in residential landscapes.

spectacle. No sooner did he arrive, though, than the female zipped toward us and crashed into the one bare spot on the window where a single ultraviolet decal among many, applied to help break the reflection, had fallen off.

We thought we'd done everything we could to mitigate hazards. We'd added full screens to the exterior of every window possible and affixed ultraviolet decals to the outside of unscreened windows. We'd put the birdbath more than thirty feet from the house so that birds would have plenty of room to maneuver if they needed to make a sudden escape. We'd grown native plants for birds rather than hanging feeders, which can draw predators who spook birds into crashing into glass at high speed. Still, it wasn't enough, and the bird found the one small patch on the lower part of our large bay window that reflected her home. I'd been planning to add another, but I'd waited too long.

The scene is repeated up to a billion times a year at homes, office buildings, and skyscrapers across the United States. Window collisions are a top source of human-caused direct mortality among wild birds. Millions more are killed when they strike automobiles, power lines, wind turbines, and communications towers, but those numbers pale in comparison to bird collisions with buildings, said Scott Loss, an associate professor at Oklahoma State University, during a talk to the local Audubon Society chapter where I volunteer.

Even when they don't die immediately from a window strike, birds hitting windows often sustain debilitating injuries. Glass confuses them not just through reflection but also through transparency, sometimes creating the impression of a continued landscape. Anyone who's walked through a screen door is familiar with the concept, though the most we usually suffer from such bumbling mistakes is a little laughter at our expense. Light pollution exacerbates the problem, interfering with migrational cues and drawing birds closer to hazards. Orienting themselves by the stars above and Earth's magnetic field, birds traveling through urban areas are especially hard hit, circling lit buildings to the point of exhaustion and becoming more vulnerable to flying into them.

But though the negative effects of high-rise buildings and displays like the 9/11 memorial lights in New York receive the most attention, individual residences and low-rise buildings are just as problematic. In a 2013 analysis in Canada, researchers found that while skyscrapers and other large buildings are implicated in the most bird deaths on

A tufted titmouse takes in the sights and sounds from a redbud in our backyard. Birds' eyes project laterally, providing a multi-angled view of food and predators.

a per-building basis, more birds cumulatively died by crashing into homes. A year later, Loss and his colleagues published similar findings in a review of US data, showing how much the residential toll adds up. "The number of bird collisions that happens at houses is one to three per year," Loss noted. In terms of sheer numbers, "that's not a big deal on an individual level, but across all the houses in the U.S., it's as big a deal as collisions with skyscrapers and other big buildings."

In the same study, the researchers identified the species most vulnerable to building collisions, including warblers, ruby-throated hummingbirds, brown creepers, painted buntings, yellow-bellied sapsuckers, catbirds, ovenbirds, and the quietly courting couple in our front yard, the wood thrushes. Other migrating birds found to be at high risk include sparrows and American woodcocks. Around homes and other low buildings with nearby habitat, year-round residents such as cardinals, robins, chickadees, and titmice sometimes collide in large numbers as well.

In recent years, scientists have been working to parse out environmental and human-made factors that contribute to building collisions, evaluating atmospheric conditions, seasonal differences, architecture, and vegetation in landscapes surrounding buildings. Stormy weather, buildings with canyon-like alcoves, nearby vegetation, and, of course, night lights and lots of glass appear to be major culprits.

Fundamentally, though, window collisions reflect the inherent conflict between the way birds and humans see the world. A bird's-eye view is really a human's side view, and only if we really stretch our eyeballs. As British ornithologist Graham Martin explained in his book *Bird Senses*, "there are many different bird's-eye views" that depend on a given species' lifestyle and habits, but no bird's eyes face forward. They project laterally, and many birds only see in front of them using the extreme periphery of their eyes' optical systems. Birds can take in more of the visual space around them, but they see it differently, often with lower resolution in front of them. When a bird foraging among the leaves in your garden tilts her head, she's getting a better look at the caterpillar she's about to catch.

"Forward-facing eyes perhaps give humans a perspective in which we experience the world as always lying ahead, not above us or behind us, and hardly to the side," Martin wrote. "This gives us the impression that we are constantly moving forwards into the world. In the

Hit by a car on our rural road, this screech owl was treated for a concussion and released back into our neighbor's five-acre wildlife habitat two weeks later.

majority of animals, and certainly in most birds, the world surrounds them, and they flow through it. As they move through their world, many birds can track an object from in front of them, past them, and watch it retreat behind them—something that is impossible for us, but which we would no doubt find very useful on occasion."

Vision in birds may have evolved more to help with foraging and detection of predators than with locomotion control, Martin suggested. In a natural setting, the airspace above plants is usually open and free of barriers, a predictable environment. Given these presumed direct flight paths, it may be more profitable for birds to survey the landscape for food and attackers than to prepare for a possible barrier they haven't evolved to even comprehend. This could explain why Will and I had a near head-on collision with a scarlet tanager one evening while sitting on a new bench by the pond. Not expecting an obstacle of big human heads on what was likely his nightly flight toward the walnut trees, the bird flew at full speed within inches of our faces before making an abrupt right turn.

Though human senses haven't evolved to handle our own modern traveling behaviors, the external systems we've put in place help us operate beyond our natural limits, Martin pointed out. Road engineering, signs, and regulations on the behaviors of drivers help make the environment more routine and predictable. "However, through the construction of our artefacts," he wrote, "we have also presented birds with many sensory challenges that go far beyond those that their senses evolved to cope with." Even our arbitrary temporal shifts in routine exacerbate hazards both at home and on the road, as we discovered when Will found a screech owl hit by a car while jogging down the street one fall. A wildlife rehabilitation organization, the Owl Moon Raptor Center, took her in and successfully treated her, but the facility was already filling up when I got there. "It's dark earlier, and the owls are out during the traffic," the director, Suzanne Shoemaker, told me as she prepared to examine our scared patient. "And we get a huge uptick as soon as the clocks turn back."

Negative consequences aren't always inevitable when we interfere with the visual landscape. On the roads we can drive more slowly. At home we can mitigate collisions by turning out the lights and making windows more visible; adhesive products like Feather Friendly, with closely spaced strips of white dots, are inconspicuous to humans but proven to break up reflections for birds. In the broader community, we can advocate for laws like the lifesaving one in New York City that requires new construction and renovations to incorporate bird-friendly design.

Outside our window, the stunned wood thrush flew away, but I'll never know if she was OK or whether her mate found her again. This is not just my home, and as long as I live, it will always belong to the birds and other wild animals whose families have lived here for generations before mine. They deserve better, here and wherever they may travel, so I've joined our local and state initiatives to make sure all our buildings are safe for them in their fractured but still beloved homeland. I've also joined the broader community of environmentalists to try to piece back together some of our wounded landscapes, ensuring that future generations of hummingbirds, wrens, fireflies, planthoppers, wasps, squirrels, butterflies, and bees have all the leaves, mosses, twigs, and other homebuilding materials they need. As we try to envision what a more humane, diverse, and welcoming community looks like, it helps to imagine the animals serving on their own HOA board or city council and channel a vision of what they would like to see. What would the world look like if we gave a vote to these nonhuman residents—and why shouldn't we?

ACKNOWLEDGMENTS

This book started, as so many projects do, with a lament: "I wish more people could perceive the world the way animals and plants do," I said one night. "Then maybe they wouldn't make so much noise."

"Why don't you write a book about that?" Will suggested. "There are lots of books about gardening for the senses. What if you write about gardening for wildlife senses?"

The themes have evolved a few times since then, but Will Heinz never lost his enthusiasm for our backyard discoveries. He also fed me when I otherwise would have forgotten to eat. I couldn't have finished without his thoughtfulness, feedback, IT support, scientific advising, and faith in me.

Science, heart, and imagination made this book possible. I'm grateful to the scientists and naturalists who pursue the nearly lost art of natural history studies and to those who take time to explain their work. Thanks especially to Michael Boppré and Dick Vane-Wright, who treated the observations of an amateur with the seriousness they deserved.

Throughout these isolating years of the pandemic, I never felt alone while writing, thanks to friends of all kinds. The humans: Carrie Allan, Eric Baratta, Mimi Bix-Hylan, Melinda Byrd, Katie Conlee-Griffin, Paula Corson, Julie Dunlap, Johanna Garrison, Toni Genberg, John Griffin, John Hadidian, Alex and Kelly Lakatos, Molly McElwee, Betsy McFarland, Angela Moxley, Raj Mukhopadhyay and Gautam Saxena, Lauren Raivel,

Cory Smith, Steph Shain, Jason Smith, Wayne Straight, and the many people I'm so lucky to have met through this work. The rest of the animal kingdom: Mr. Chippie, my green frog friends, the birds who explored alongside me, my insect teachers, and countless others.

Online collaboration with Howard County Bee City friends—especially Julie Costantino, Kevin Heffernan, and Susan Tucker—gave me something to look forward to during the weeks I worked largely alone. I'm grateful also to the organizations around the country that invited me to speak, keeping me connected virtually with nature lovers and keeping hope alive.

Thanks to all the photographers who notice the little things that run the world; to the incomparable Michelle Riley for her photo-editing tips; and to Kelly Williams, who reviewed several chapter drafts and provided insightful, honest feedback.

Sara Stemen's patience with my delays, questions, and second-guessing was only matched by her uncanny ability to put me back on track with just a few words of perceptive direction, edits, and encouragement. She is a Yoda, thoughtfully balancing deadlines and author fussiness without ever losing her cool. I'm excited to have another book graced by Ben English's artistry. Thanks to everyone else at Princeton Architectural Press who helped bring *Wildscape* to fruition.

Loreen, Eric, Nora, Conrad, Karl, Corinna, and the rest of the extended Heinz family: you brought song and joy by the firepits. To Mary, Jeff, and India Lawson and to Janet, Jeff, and Elise Crouch: I treasure our mutual appreciation for flowers, talking animals, and walking trees. To Daddy, Aunt Sharon, and sweet nephew Ryan, I miss you, but I listen for your voices each morning, rising with the wrens to greet us.

Chapter 1

Boachon, Benoît, C. Robin Buell, Emily Crisovan, et al. "Phylogenomic Mining of the Mints Reveals Multiple Mechanisms Contributing to the Evolution of Chemical Diversity in Lamiaceae." *Molecular Plant* 11, no. 8 (2018): 1084–96.

Boppré, Michael. "Leaf-Scratching: A Specialized Behaviour of Danaine Butterflies (Lepidoptera) for Gathering Secondary Plant Substances." *Oecologia* 59, no. 2 (1983): 414–16.

Boppré, Michael, and Steven M. Colegate. "Recognition of Pyrrolizidine Alkaloid Esters in the Invasive Aquatic Plant Gymnocoronis Spilanthoides (Asteraceae)." *Phytochemical Analysis* 26, no. 3 (2015): 215–25.

Bushdid, C., M. O. Magnasco, L. B. Vosshall, and A. Keller. "Humans Can Discriminate More Than One Trillion Olfactory Stimuli." *Science* 343, no. 6177 (2014): 1370–72.

Cardé, Ring T., and Mark A. Willis. "Navigational Strategies Used by Insects to Find Distant, Wind-Borne Sources of Odor." *Journal of Chemical Ecology* 34, no. 7 (2008): 854–66.

Childs, Craig. *The Animal Dialogues: Uncommon Encounters in the Wild.* New York: Little Brown, 2007.

Diehl, Robert H., Anna C. Peterson, Rachel T. Bolus, and Douglas H. Johnson. "Extending the Habitat Concept to the Airspace." In *Aeroecology* (Cham, Switzerland: Springer, 2017): 47–69.

Doody, J. Sean, Vladimir Dinets, and Gordon Burghardt, eds. *The Secret Social Lives of Reptiles*. Baltimore: Johns Hopkins University Press, 2021.

Fuentes, Jose D., Marcelo Chamecki, T'ai Roulston, Bicheng Chen, and Kenneth R. Pratt. "Air Pollutants Degrade Floral Scents and Increase Insect Foraging Times." *Atmospheric Environment* 141 (2016): 361–74.

Girling, Robbie D., Inka Lusebrink, Emily Farthing, Tracey A. Newman, and Guy M. Poppy. "Diesel Exhaust Rapidly Degrades Floral Odours Used by Honeybees." *Scientific Reports* 3, no. 2779 (2013).

Hoyt, Erich, and Ted Schultz, eds. *Insects Lives: Stories of Mystery and Romance from a Hidden World*. New York: John Wiley & Sons, 1999.

Keefover-Ring, Ken. "Chemotype Distribution of Monarda on City of Boulder Open Space and Mountain Parks Lands." 2008.

———. "Making Scents of Defense: Do Fecal Shields and Herbivore-Caused Volatiles Match Host Plant Chemical Profiles?" *Chemoecology* 23, no. 1 (2013).

———. "Monarda Fistulosa: Making Good Scents in Colorado." *Aquilegia* 30, no. 2 (2006): 3–4.

Lawson, Nancy, Richard I. Vane-Wright, and Michael Boppré. "The Puzzle of Monarch Butterflies (*Danaus plexippus*) and Their Association with Plants Containing Pyrrolizidine Alkaloids." *Ecological Entomology* 46, no. 5 (2021): 999–1005.

McFrederick, Quinn S., James C. Kathilankal, and Jose D. Fuentes. "Air Pollution Modifies Floral Scent Trails." *Atmospheric Environment* 42, no. 10 (2008): 2336–48.

McGee, Harold. *Nose Dive: A Field Guide to the World's Smells*. New York: Penguin, 2020.

Ramos, Bruna de Cássia Menezes, José Roberto Trigo, and Daniela Rodrigues. "Danaus Butterflies of the Americas Do Not Perform Leaf-Scratching." *Arthropod-Plant Interactions* 14, no. 4 (2020): 521–29.

Sprayberry, Jordanna D. H. "Compounds without Borders: A Mechanism for Quantifying Complex Odors and Responses to Scent-Pollution in Bumblebees." *PLoS Computational Biology* 16, no. 4 (2020).

———. "The Prevalence of Olfactory versus Visual-Signal Encounter by Searching Bumblebees." *Scientific Reports* 8, no. 1 (2018).

Weiss, Martha R. "Defecation Behavior and Ecology of Insects." *Annual Review of Entomology* 51 (2006): 635–61.

———. "Good Housekeeping: Why Do Shelter-Dwelling Caterpillars Fling Their Frass?" *Ecology Letters* 6, no. 4 (2003): 361–70.

Wilson, J. Keaton, André Kessler, and H. Arthur Woods. "Noisy Communication via Airborne Infochemicals." *BioScience* 65, no. 7 (2015): 667–77.

Chapter 2

Appel, H. M., and R. B. Cocroft. "Plants Respond to Leaf Vibrations Caused by Insect Herbivore Chewing." *Oecologia* 175, no. 4 (2014): 1257–66.

Aschemeier, Lisa M., and Christine R. Maher. "Eavesdropping of Woodchucks (Marmota Monax) and Eastern Chipmunks (Tamias Striatus) on Heterospecific Alarm Calls." *Journal of Mammalogy* 92, no. 3 (2011): 493–99.

Bee, Mark A., Stephen A. Perrill, and Patrick C. Owen. "Male Green Frogs Lower the Pitch of Acoustic Signals in Defense of Territories: A Possible Dishonest Signal of Size?" *Behavioral Ecology* 11, no. 2 (2000): 169–77.

Bee, Mark A., and Eli M. Swanson. "Auditory Masking of Anuran Advertisement Calls by Road Traffic Noise." *Animal Behaviour* 74, no. 6 (2007): 1765–76.

Bunkley, Jessie P., Christopher J. W. McClure, Akito Y. Kawahara, Clinton D. Francis, and Jesse R. Barber. "Anthropogenic Noise Changes Arthropod Abundances." *Ecology and Evolution* 7, no. 9 (2017): 2977–85.

Bunkley, Jessie P., Christopher J. W. McClure, Nathan J. Kleist, Clinton D. Francis, and Jesse R. Barber. "Anthropogenic Noise Alters Bat Activity Levels and Echolocation Calls." *Global Ecology and Conservation* 3 (January 2015): 62–71.

Burke da Silva, Karen, Donald L. Kramer, and Daniel M. Weary. "Context-Specific Alarm Calls of the Eastern Chipmunk, *Tamias striatus*." *Canadian Journal of Zoology* 72, no. 6 (1994): 1087–92.

Burke da Silva, Karen, Carolyn Mahan, and Jack da Silva. "The Trill of the Chase: Eastern Chipmunks Call to Warn Kin." *Journal of Mammalogy* 83, no. 2 (2002): 546–52.

Chiu, Chen, Wei Xian, and Cynthia F. Moss. "Flying in Silence: Echolocating Bats Cease Vocalizing to Avoid Sonar Jamming." *Proceedings of the National Academy of Sciences* 105, no. 35 (2008): 13116–21.

Corbani, Tayanne L., Jessica E. Martin, and Susan D. Healy. "The Impact of Acute Loud Noise on the Behavior of Laboratory Birds." *Frontiers in Veterinary Science* 7 (2021): 1134.

Corcoran, Aaron J., Theodore J. Weller, Annalise Hopkins, and Yossi Yovel. "Silence and Reduced Echolocation during Flight Are Associated with Social Behaviors in Male Hoary Bats (*Lasiurus cinereus*)." *Scientific Reports* 11, no. 1 (2021).

Davis, Andrew K., Hayley Schroeder, Ian Yeager, and Jana Pearce. "Effects of Simulated Highway Noise on Heart Rates of Larval Monarch Butterflies, *Danaus plexippus*: Implications for Roadside Habitat Suitability." *Biology Letters* 14, no. 5 (2018).

de Sá, Fábio P., Juliana Zina, and Celio F. B. Haddad. "Sophisticated Communication in the Brazilian Torrent Frog *Hylodes japi*." *PLoS ONE* 11, no. 1 (2016).

Derryberry, Elizabeth P., Jennifer N. Phillips, Graham E. Derryberry, Michael J. Blum, and David Luther. "Singing in a Silent Spring: Birds Respond to a Half-Century Soundscape Reversion during the COVID-19 Shutdown." *Science* 370, no. 6516 (2020): 575–79.

Dowling, J. L., D. A. Luther, and P. P. Marra. "Comparative Effects of Urban Development and Anthropogenic Noise on Bird Songs." *Behavioral Ecology* 23, no. 1 (2012): 201–9.

Elliott, Lang. "Social Behavior and Foraging Ecology of the Eastern Chipmunk (*Tamias striatus*) in the Adirondack Mountains." *Smithsonian Contributions to Zoology*, no. 265 (1978).

Ferraro, Danielle M., Zachary D. Miller, Lauren A. Ferguson, et al. "The Phantom Chorus: Birdsong Boosts Human Well-Being in Protected Areas: Phantom Chorus Improves Human Well-Being." *Proceedings of the Royal Society B: Biological Sciences* 287, no. 1941 (2020).

WILDSCAPE

Francis, Clinton D., Nathan J. Kleist, Catherine P. Ortega, and Alexander Cruz. "Noise Pollution Alters Ecological Services: Enhanced Pollination and Disrupted Seed Dispersal." *Proceedings of the Royal Society B: Biological Sciences* 279, no. 1739 (2012): 2727–35.

Francis, Clinton D., Peter Newman, B. Derrick Taff, et al. "Acoustic Environments Matter: Synergistic Benefits to Humans and Ecological Communities." *Journal of Environmental Management* 203 (2017): 245–54.

Francis, Clinton D., Juan Paritsis, Catherine P. Ortega, and Alexander Cruz. "Landscape Patterns of Avian Habitat Use and Nest Success Are Affected by Chronic Gas Well Compressor Noise." *Landscape Ecology* 26, no. 9 (2011): 1269–80.

Gentry, Katherine E., Megan F. McKenna, and David A. Luther. "Evidence of Suboscine Song Plasticity in Response to Traffic Noise Fluctuations and Temporary Road Closures." *Bioacoustics* 27, no. 2 (2018): 165–81.

Grunst, Melissa L., Andrea S. Grunst, Rianne Pinxten, and Marcel Eens. "Variable and Consistent Traffic Noise Negatively Affect the Sleep Behavior of a Free-Living Songbird." *Science of the Total Environment* 778 (2021).

Haines, Casey D., Evangeline M. Rose, Karan J. Odom, and Kevin E. Omland. "The Role of Diversity in Science: A Case Study of Women Advancing Female Birdsong Research." *Animal Behaviour* 168 (2020): 19–24.

Kafash, Zohreh Haghighi, Shahrzad Khoramnejadian, Ali Akbar Ghotbi-Ravandi, and Somayeh Farhang Dehghan. "Traffic Noise Induces Oxidative Stress and Phytohormone Imbalance in Two Urban Plant Species." *Basic and Applied Ecology* 60 (2022).

Kazo, Laura. "Avian Responses to Different Anthropogenic Disturbances and Habitats." Master's thesis, George Mason University, 2021.

Keizer, Garret. *The Unwanted Sound of Everything We Want: A Book about Noise.* New York: PublicAffairs, 2010.

Khait, I., U. Obolski, Y. Yovel, and L. Hadany. "Sound Perception in Plants." *Seminars in Cell and Developmental Biology* 92 (2019): 134–38.

Kleist, Nathan J., Robert P. Guralnick, Alexander Cruz, and Clinton D. Francis. "Anthropogenic Noise Weakens Territorial Response to Intruder's Songs." *Ecosphere* 7, no. 3 (2016).

Kleist, Nathan J., Robert P. Guralnick, Alexander Cruz, Christopher A. Lowry, and Clinton D. Francis. "Chronic Anthropogenic Noise Disrupts Glucocorticoid Signaling and Has Multiple Effects on Fitness in an Avian Community." *Proceedings of the National Academy of Sciences* 115, no. 4 (2018).

Krause, Bernie. *Voices of the Wild: Animal Songs, Human Din, and the Call to Save Natural Soundscapes.* New Haven, CT: Yale University Press, 2015.

Leavell, Brian C., Juliette J. Rubin, Christopher J. W. McClure, Krystie A. Miner, Marc A. Branham, and Jesse R. Barber. "Fireflies Thwart Bat Attack with Multisensory Warnings." *Science Advances* 4, no. 8 (2018).

Luther, David A., and Jessica Magnotti. "Can Animals Detect Differences in Vocalizations Adjusted for Anthropogenic Noise?" *Animal Behaviour* 92 (2014): 111–16.

Luther, David A., Jennifer Phillips, and Elizabeth P. Derryberry. "Not So Sexy in the City: Urban Birds Adjust Songs to Noise but Compromise Vocal Performance." *Behavioral Ecology* 27, no. 1 (2016): 332–40.

Mandelbaum, Ryan F. "This Winter Marks an Incredible 'Superflight' of Hungry Winter Finches." *Audubon*, December 11, 2021. https://www.audubon.org/news/this-winter-marks-incredible-superflight-hungry-winter-finches.

McCann Worldgroup. "Today's Global Youth Would Give Up Their Sense of Smell to Keep Their Technology." *PR Newswire*, May 25, 2011. https://prn.to/3alAnSq.

McClure, Christopher J. W., Heidi E. Ware, Jay Carlisle, Gregory Kaltenecker, and Jesse R. Barber. "An Experimental Investigation into the Effects of Traffic Noise on Distributions of Birds: Avoiding the Phantom Road." *Proceedings of the Royal Society B: Biological Sciences* 280, no. 1773 (2013).

Mooney, Bridget, and Macy Wannamaker. "A Case Study of the Eviction of a Female Bobcat and Her Four Kittens from a Suburban Backyard in Fremont, California." *Proceedings of the Vertebrate Pest Conference* 29, no. 29 (2020).

Munn, Charles A. "Birds That 'Cry Wolf.'" *Nature* 319, no. 6049 (1986): 143–45.

Parris, Kirsten M., Meah Velik-Lord, and Joanne M. A. North. "Frogs Call at a Higher Pitch in Traffic Noise." *Ecology and Society* 14, no. 1 (2009).

Phillips, Jennifer N., and Elizabeth P. Derryberry. "Urban Sparrows Respond to a Sexually Selected Trait with Increased Aggression in Noise." *Scientific Reports* 8, no. (2018).

Phillips, Jennifer N., Katherine E. Gentry, David A. Luther, and Elizabeth P. Derryberry. "Surviving in the City: Higher Apparent Survival for Urban Birds but Worse Condition on Noisy Territories." *Ecosphere* 9, no. 9 (2018).

Phillips, Jennifer N., Sophia K. Ruef, Christopher M. Garvin, My Lan T. Le, and Clinton D. Francis. "Background Noise Disrupts Host-Parasitoid Interactions." *Royal Society Open Science* 6, no. 9 (2019).

Phillips, Jennifer N., Sarah E. Termondt, and Clinton D. Francis. "Long-Term Noise Pollution Affects Seedling Recruitment and Community Composition, with Negative Effects Persisting after Removal." *Proceedings of the Royal Society B: Biological Sciences* 288, no. 1948 (2021).

Schrimpf, Michael B., Paulson G. Des Brisay, Alison Johnston, et al. "Reduced Human Activity during COVID-19 Alters Avian Land Use across North America." *Science Advances* 7, no. 39 (2021).

Shannon, Delisa, and Noah Friedman. "Teens Would Rather Break Their Bones Than Lose Their Phones." *Business Insider*, May 6, 2021.

Shannon, Graeme, Lisa M. Angeloni, George Wittemyer, Kurt M. Fristrup, and Kevin R. Crooks. "Road Traffic Noise Modifies Behaviour of a Keystone Species." *Animal Behaviour* 94 (2014): 135–41.

Shannon, Graeme, Megan F. McKenna, Grete E. Wilson-Henjum, Lisa M. Angeloni, Kevin R. Crooks, and George Wittemyer. "Vocal Characteristics of Prairie Dog Alarm Calls across an Urban Noise Gradient." *Behavioral Ecology* 31, no. 2 (2020): 393–400.

Stocker, Michael. *Hear Where We Are: Sound, Ecology, and Sense of Place.* New York: Springer, 2013.

Tan, W. H., C. G. Tsai, C. Lin, and Y. K. Lin. "Urban Canyon Effect: Storm Drains Enhance Call Characteristics of the Mientien Tree Frog." *Journal of Zoology* 294, no. 2 (2014): 77–84.

Vargas-Salinas, Fernando, Glenn M. Cunnington, Adolfo Amézquita, and Lenore Fahrig. "Does Traffic Noise Alter Calling Time in Frogs and Toads? A Case Study of Anurans in Eastern Ontario, Canada." *Urban Ecosystems* 17, no. 4 (2014): 945–53.

Veits, Marine, Itzhak Khait, Uri Obolski, et al. "Flowers Respond to Pollinator Sound within Minutes by Increasing Nectar Sugar Concentration." *Ecology Letters* 22, no. 9 (2019): 1483–92.

Williams, Danielle P., Julian D. Avery, Thomas B. Gabrielson, and Margaret C. Brittingham. "Experimental Playback of Natural Gas Compressor Noise Reduces Incubation Time and Hatching Success in Two Secondary Cavity-Nesting Bird Species." *Condor* 123, no. 1 (2021).

Chapter 3

Abrahamczyk, Stefan, and Susanne S. Renner. "The Temporal Build-up of Hummingbird/Plant Mutualisms in North America and Temperate South America." *BMC Evolutionary Biology* 15, no. 1 (2015).

Ali, Jared G., and Anurag A. Agrawal. "Asymmetry of Plant-Mediated Interactions between Specialist Aphids and Caterpillars on Two Milkweeds." *Functional Ecology* 28, no. 6 (2014): 1404–12.

Avalos, Gerardo. "What's the Impact of Hummingbird Feeders?" *The School for Field Studies* (blog), February 7, 2012. https://fieldstudies.org/2012/02/whats-the-impact-of-hummingbird-feeders/.

Avalos, Gerardo, Alejandra Soto, and Willy Alfaro. "Effect of Artificial Feeders on Pollen Loads of the Hummingbirds of Cerro de La Muerte, Costa Rica." *Revista de Biologia Tropical* 60, no. 1 (2012): 65–73.

Bergman, Margareta. "Can Saliva from Moose, *Alces alces*, Affect Growth Responses in the Sallow, *Salix caprea*?" *Oikos* 96, no. 1 (2002): 164–68.

Boggs, Carol L., and Lee Ann Jackson. "Mud Puddling by Butterflies Is Not a Simple Matter." *Ecological Entomology* 16, no. 1 (1991): 123–27.

Buono, Carmela. "Ant-Mediated Seed Dispersal in Contemporary Forests." Torrey Botanical Society, posted April 1, 2021. YouTube video, 1:10:40. https://www.youtube.com/watch?v=DWP57nqldl4.

———. "Land Use History Effects on Ant-Mediated Seed Dispersal: Reduction of a Key Ecosystem Function in Secondary Deciduous Forests." Ecological Society of America Annual Meeting, August 4, 2020.

Burger, Joanna, and Michael Gochfeld. "Smooth-Billed Ani (Crotophaga ani) Predation on Butterflies in Mato Grosso, Brazil: Risk Decreases with Increased Group Size." *Behavioral Ecology and Sociobiology* 49, no. 6 (2001): 482–92.

Burghardt, Karin T. "Nutrient Supply Alters Goldenrod's Induced Response to Herbivory." *Functional Ecology* 30, no. 11 (2016): 1769–78.

Cane, James H., and Vincent J. Tepedino. "Gauging the Effect of Honey Bee Pollen Collection on Native Bee Communities." *Conservation Letters* 10, no. 2 (2017): 205–10.

Collie, Joseph, Odelvys Granela, Elizabeth B. Brown, and Alex C. Keene. "Aggression Is Induced by Resource Limitation in the Monarch Caterpillar." *iScience* 23, no. 12 (2020).

Davis, Andrew K., and Cody Prouty. "The Sicker the Better: Nematode-Infected Passalus Beetles Provide Enhanced Ecosystem Services." *Biology Letters* 15, no. 5 (2019).

de la Rosa, Carlos L. "Additional Observations of Lachryphagous Butterflies and Bees." *Frontiers in Ecology and the Environment* 12, no. 4 (2014): 210.

del Coro Arizmendi, María, Constanza Monterrubio Solís, Lourdes Juárez, Ivonne Flores-Moreno, and Edgar Gustavo López-Saut. "Effect of the Presence of Nectar Feeders on the Breeding Success of Salvia mexicana and Salvia fulgens in a Suburban Park near Mexico City." *Biological Conservation* 136, no. 1 (2007): 155–58.

Dunn, Rob. *Never Home Alone*. New York: Basic Books, 2018.

Eisner, Thomas, Maria Eisner, and Melody Siegler. *Secret Weapons: Defenses of Insects, Spiders, Scorpions, and Other Many-Legged Creatures*. Cambridge, MA: Harvard University Press, 2005.

Evans, Art. *Beetles of Eastern North America*. Princeton, NJ: Princeton University Press, 2014.

Fricke, Evan C., Alejandro Ordonez, Haldre S. Rogers, and Jens-Christian Svenning. "The Effects of Defaunation on Plants' Capacity to Track Climate Change." *Science* 375, no. 6577 (2022): 210–14.

Grinath, Joshua B., Brian D. Inouye, and Nora Underwood. "Bears Benefit Plants via a Cascade with Both Antagonistic and Mutualistic Interactions." *Ecology Letters* 18, no. 2 (2015): 164–73.

Hafernik, John, and Leslie Saul-Gershenz. "Beetle Larvae Cooperate to Mimic Bees." *Nature* 405, no. 6782 (2000): 35–36.

Hatfield, Richard, Sarina Jepsen, Mace Vaughan, Scott Black, and Eric Lee-Mäder. "An Overview of the Potential Impacts of Honey Bees to Native Bees, Plant Communities, and Ecosystems in Wild Landscapes: Recommendations for Land Managers." Portland, OR: The Xerces Society for Invertebrate Conservation, 2018.

Hay, Mark E. "Associational Plant Defenses and the Maintenance of Species Diversity: Turning Competitors into Accomplices." *American Naturalist* 128, no. 5 (1986): 617–41.

Himanen, Sari J., James D. Blande, Tero Klemola, Juha Pulkkinen, Juha Heijari, and Jarmo K. Holopainen. "Birch (Betula Spp.) Leaves Adsorb and Re-Release Volatiles Specific to Neighbouring Plants—a Mechanism for Associational Herbivore Resistance?" *New Phytologist* 186, no. 3 (2010): 722–32.

Karban, Richard, Carrie A. Black, and Steven A. Weinbaum. "How Seventeen-Year Cicadas Keep Track of Time." *Ecology Letters* 3, no. 4 (2000): 253–56.

Kaspari, Michael. "Road Salt Offers Insights into the Connections between Diet and Neural Development." *Proceedings of the National Academy of Sciences of the United States of America* 111, no. 28 (2014).

Kaspari, Michael, Stephen P. Yanoviak, and Robert Dudley. "On the Biogeography of Salt Limitation: A Study of Ant Communities." *Proceedings of the National Academy of Sciences* 105, no. 46 (2008): 17848–51.

Knight, Tiffany M., Michael W. McCoy, Jonathan M. Chase, Krista A. McCoy, and Robert D. Holt. "Trophic Cascades across Ecosystems." *Nature* 437, no. 7060 (2005): 880–83.

Kumar, Pavan, Erandi Vargas Ortiz, Etzel Garrido, Katja Poveda, and Georg Jander. "Potato Tuber Herbivory Increases Resistance to Aboveground Lepidopteran Herbivores." *Oecologia* 182, no. 1 (2016): 177–87.

Lash, Chloe, Melissa Cregger, and Charles Kwit. "Seed-Dispersing Ants Alter Seed Coat Microbiomes." Ecological Society of America Annual Meeting, August 4, 2020.

Lin, Qianshi, Cécile Ané, Thomas J. Givnish, and Sean W. Graham. "A New Carnivorous Plant Lineage (Triantha) with a Unique Sticky-Inflorescence Trap." *Proceedings of the National Academy of Sciences of the United States of America* 118, no. 33 (2021).

Ohse, Bettina, Almuth Hammerbacher, Carolin Seele, et al. "Salivary Cues: Simulated Roe Deer Browsing Induces Systemic Changes in Phytohormones and Defence Chemistry in Wild-Grown Maple and Beech Saplings." *Functional Ecology* 31, no. 2 (2017): 340–49.

Parker, Wyatt J., Carmela M. Buono, and Kirsten M. Prior. "Antagonistic and Mutualistic Interactions Alter Seed Dispersal of Understory Plants at Forest Edges." *Ecosphere* 12, no. 3 (2021).

Pennisi, Elizabeth. "Don't Crush That Ant—It Could Plant a Wildflower." *Science*, August 11, 2020.

Ramula, Satu, Ken N. Paige, Tommy Lennartsson, and Juha Tuomi. "Overcompensation: A Thirty-Year Perspective." *Ecology* 100, no. 5 (2019).

Ravenscraft, Alison, and Carol L. Boggs. "Nutrient Acquisition across a Dietary Shift: Fruit Feeding Butterflies Crave Amino Acids, Nectivores Seek Salt." *Oecologia* 181, no. 1 (2016).

Reilly, J. R., D. R. Artz, D. Biddinger, et al. "Crop Production in the USA Is Frequently Limited by a Lack of Pollinators." *Proceedings of the Royal Society B: Biological Sciences* 287, no. 1931 (2020).

Rivest, Sébastien, and Jessica R. K. Forrest. "Defence Compounds in Pollen: Why Do They Occur and How Do They Affect the Ecology and Evolution of Bees?" *New Phytologist* 225, no. 3 (2020): 1053–64.

Rooke, Tuulikki. "Growth Responses of a Woody Species to Clipping and Goat Saliva." *African Journal of Ecology* 41, no. 4 (2003): 324–28.

Saul-Gershenz, Leslie, and Jocelyn G. Millar. "Phoretic Nest Parasites Use Sexual Deception to Obtain Transport to Their Host's Nest." *Proceedings of the National Academy of Sciences* 103, no. 38 (2006): 14039–44.

Saul-Gershenz, Leslie, and Mandy L. Heddle. "New Records of Pedilus (Coleoptera: Pyrochroidae) on Meloe Strigulosus Mannerheim 1852 (Coleoptera: Meloidae)." *Pan Pacific Entomologist* 80, no. 1–4 (2004): 18–22.

Sculley, Colleen E., and Carol L. Boggs. "Mating Systems and Sexual Division of Foraging Effort Affect Puddling Behaviour by Butterflies." *Ecological Entomology* 21, no. 2 (1996): 193–97.

Shakeri, Yasaman N., Kevin S. White, and Taal Levi. "Salmon-Supported Bears, Seed Dispersal, and Extensive Resource Subsidies to Granivores." *Ecosphere* 9, no. 6 (2018).

Snell-Rood, Emilie C., Anne Espeset, Christopher J. Boser, William A. White, and Rhea Smykalski. "Anthropogenic Changes in Sodium Affect Neural and Muscle Development in Butterflies." *Proceedings of the National Academy of Sciences* 111, no. 28 (2014): 10221–26.

Stevenson, Misty, Kalynn L. Hudman, Alyx Scott, Kelsey Contreras, and Jeffrey G. Kopachena. "High Survivorship of First-Generation Monarch Butterfly Eggs to Third Instar Associated with a Diverse Arthropod Community." *Insects* 12, no. 6 (2021).

Stokstad, Erik. "Loss of Seed-Hauling Animals Spells Trouble for Plants in Warming World." *Science*, January 13, 2022.

Stuble, Katharine L., and Sergio A. Sabat-Bonilla. "Ant-Mediated Seed Dispersal in Today's Forests: How Agricultural Abandonment and Earthworm Invasion Are Driving Seed Dispersal." Ecological Society of America Annual Meeting, August 4, 2020.

Tewksbury, Joshua J., and Gary P. Nabhan. "Directed Deterrence by Capsaicin in Chillies." *Nature* 412, no. 6845 (2001): 403–4.

Thomsen, Philip Francis, and Eva E. Sigsgaard. "Environmental DNA Metabarcoding of Wild Flowers Reveals Diverse Communities of Terrestrial Arthropods." *Ecology and Evolution* 9, no. 4 (2019): 1665–79.

Thomson, Diane M. "Local Bumble Bee Decline Linked to Recovery of Honey Bees, Drought Effects on Floral Resources." *Ecology Letters* 19, no. 10 (2016): 1247–55.

Torres, Phil. "Butterflies Drinking Turtle Tears!?" The Jungle Diaries. Posted July 14, 2018. YouTube video, 3:00. www.youtube.com/watch?v=4Dj78JCKlPU.

Travis, Dillon J., and Joshua R. Kohn. "Super Abundant, Non-Native Honey Bees *(Apis Mellifera)* Decrease the Fitness of Native, Coastal Sage Scrub Plants in Southern California." Ecological Society of America Annual Meeting, August 2, 2021.

Vaudo, Anthony D., Harland M. Patch, David A. Mortensen, John F. Tooker, and Christina M. Grozinger. "Macronutrient Ratios in Pollen Shape Bumble Bee (Bombus impatiens) Foraging Strategies and Floral Preferences." *Proceedings of the National Academy of Sciences* 113, no. 28 (2016).

Wagner, David L. *Caterpillars of Eastern North America*. Princeton, NJ: Princeton University Press, 2005.

Chapter 4

Broughton, Richard K., James M. Bullock, Charles George, et al. "Long-Term Woodland Restoration on Lowland Farmland through Passive Rewilding." *PloS ONE* 16, no. 6 (2021).

Broughton, Richard K., James M. Bullock, Charles George, et al. "Slow Development of Woodland Vegetation and Bird Communities during Thirty-Three Years of Passive Rewilding in Open Farmland." Manuscript submitted for publication, 2022.

Coverdale, Tyler C., Jacob R. Goheen, Todd M. Palmer, and Robert M. Pringle. "Good Neighbors Make Good Defenses: Associational Refuges Reduce Defense Investment in African Savanna Plants." *Ecology* 99, no. 8 (2018): 1724–36.

Cronberg, Nils, Rayna Natcheva, and Katarina Hedlund. "Microarthropods Mediate Sperm Transfer in Mosses." *Science* 313, no. 5791 (2006): 1255.

Davis, Andrew K. "Evaluating Cardiac Reactions of Monarch Butterflies to Human Handling across Three Life Stages." *Journal of the Lepidopterists' Society* 74, no. 1 (2020): 43–50.

Eaton, Eric. *Wasps: The Astonishing Diversity of a Misunderstood Insect.* Princeton, NJ: Princeton University Press, 2021.

Elliott, Lang. "Social Behavior and Foraging Ecology of the Eastern Chipmunk (Tamias striatus) in the Adirondack Mountains." Washington, DC: *Smithsonian Contributions to Zoology*, no. 265 (1978).

Ellison, George. "The Forlorn Calls of the Yellow-Billed Cuckoo." *Smoky Mountain News*, May 2, 2018.

Fink, Tom, Vijay Ramalingam, John Seiner, Niels Skals, and Douglas Streett. "Buzz Digging and Buzz Plastering in the Black-and-Yellow Mud Dauber Wasp, Sceliphron caementarium (Drury)." *Journal of the Acoustical Society of America* 122, no. 5 (2007): 2947–48.

Gilding, Edward K., Sina Jami, Jennifer R. Deuis, et al. "Neurotoxic Peptides from the Venom of the Giant Australian Stinging Tree." *Science Advances* 6, no. 38 (2020).

Goodwin, Sarah E., and W. Gregory Shriver. "Effects of Traffic Noise on Occupancy Patterns of Forest Birds." *Conservation Biology* 25, no. 2 (2011): 406–11.

Hanski, Ilkka, Leena von Hertzen, Nanna Fyhrquist, et al. "Environmental Biodiversity, Human Microbiota, and Allergy Are Interrelated." *Proceedings of the National Academy of Sciences* 109, no. 21 (2012): 8334–39.

Holm, Heather. *Wasps: Their Biology, Diversity, and Role as Beneficial Insects and Pollinators of Native Plants*. Minnetonka, MN: Pollination Press LLC, 2021.

Kimmerer, Robin Wall. *Gathering Moss: A Natural and Cultural History of Mosses*. Corvallis: Oregon State University Press, 2003.

Kimmerer, Robin Wall, and Craig C. Young. "Effect of Gap Size and Regeneration Niche on Species Coexistence in Bryophyte Communities." *Bulletin of the Torrey Botanical Club* 123, no. 1 (1996): 16–24.

Maloof, Joan. *Teaching the Trees: Lessons from the Forest*. Athens: University of Georgia Press, 2005.

Mancuso, Stefano. *The Nation of Plants*. New York: Other Press, 2021.

Rosenstiel, Todd N., Erin E. Shortlidge, Andrea N. Melnychenko, James F. Pankow, and Sarah M. Eppley. "Sex-Specific Volatile Compounds Influence Microarthropod-Mediated Fertilization of Moss." *Nature* 489, no. 7416 (2012): 431–33.

Roulston, T'ai. "'Got a Little Love for a Deadly Nightshade?'" *Arbor Vitae: Newsletter of the Foundation of the State Arboretum*, Winter 2018.

Schmidt, Justin O. *The Sting of the Wild*. Baltimore: Johns Hopkins University Press, 2016.

Schmitz, Oswald J. *The New Ecology: Rethinking a Science for the Anthropocene.* Princeton, NJ: Princeton University Press, 2016.

Simard, Suzanne. *Finding the Mother Tree: Discovering the Wisdom of the Forest.* New York: Alfred A. Knopf, 2021.

Stephens, Ryan B., and Rebecca J. Rowe. "The Underappreciated Role of Rodent Generalists in Fungal Spore Dispersal Networks." *Ecology* 101, no. 4 (2020).

Tree, Isabella. *Wilding: The Return of Nature to a British Farm.* London: Picador, 2018.

Chapter 5

Abrahamczyk, Stefan, and Susanne S. Renner. "The Temporal Build-Up of Hummingbird/Plant Mutualisms in North America and Temperate South America." *BMC Evolutionary Biology* 15, no. 1 (2015).

Bartlett, Charles R., Lois B. O'Brien, and Stephen W. Wilson. "A Review of the Planthoppers: Hemiptera (Fulgoroidea) of the United States." *Memoirs of the American Entomological Society* 50 (2014).

Bergamo, Pedro J., André R. Rech, Vinícius L. G. Brito, and Marlies Sazima. "Flower Colour and Visitation Rates of Costus Arabicus Support the 'Bee Avoidance' Hypothesis for Red-Reflecting Hummingbird-Pollinated Flowers." *Functional Ecology* 30, no. 5 (2016): 710–20.

Canfield, Michael R., Sue Chang, and Naomi E. Pierce. "The Double Cloak of Invisibility: Phenotypic Plasticity and Larval Decoration in a Geometrid Moth, *Synchlora frondaria*, across Three Diet Treatments: Short Communication." *Ecological Entomology* 34, no. 3 (2009): 412–14.

Cornelisse, Tara, Sarina Jepsen, Candace Fallon, and Jess Tyler. "Petition for Emergency Listing of the Bethany Beach Firefly *(Photuris bethaniensis)* under the Endangered Species Act and to Concurrently Designate Critical Habitat," submitted to the US Fish and Wildlife Service, May 15, 2019.

Davranoglou, Leonidas-Romanos, Alice Cicirello, Graham K. Taylor, and Beth Mortimer. "Planthopper Bugs Use a Fast, Cyclic Elastic Recoil Mechanism for Effective Vibrational Communication at Small Body Size." *PLoS biology* 17, no. 3 (2019).

Doering, Kathleen. "The Genus Acanalonia in America North of Mexico." *Annals of the Entomological Society of America* 25, no. 4 (1932): 758–86.

Fallon, Candace E., Sarah Hoyle, Sara Lewis, et al. "Conserving the Jewels of the Night Guidelines for Protecting Fireflies in the United States and Canada." Portland, OR: Xerces Society for Invertebrate Conservation, 2019.

Fallon, Candace E., Anna C. Walker, Sara Lewis, et al. "Evaluating Firefly Extinction Risk: Initial Red List Assessments for North America." *PLoS ONE* 16, no. 11 (2021).

Faust, Lynn Frierson. *Fireflies, Glow-Worms, and Lightning Bugs: Identification and Natural History of the Fireflies of the Eastern and Central United States and Canada.* Athens: University of Georgia Press, 2017.

Hager, Stephen B., Bradley J. Cosentino, Miguel A. Aguilar-Gómez, et al. "Continent-Wide Analysis of How Urbanization Affects Bird-Window Collision Mortality in North America." *Biological Conservation* 212 (2017): 209–15.

Hogan, Benedict G., and Mary Caswell Stoddard. "Synchronization of Speed, Sound and Iridescent Color in a Hummingbird Aerial Courtship Dive." *Nature Communications* 9, no. 1 (2018).

Laraba, Imane, Susan P. McCormick, Martha M. Vaughan, et al. "Pseudoflowers Produced by Fusarium Xyrophilum on Yellow-Eyed Grass (*Xyris* Spp.) in Guyana: A Novel Floral Mimicry System?" *Fungal Genetics and Biology* 144 (2020).

Leonard, Anne S., Joshua Brent, Daniel R. Papaj, and Anna Dornhaus. "Floral Nectar Guide Patterns Discourage Nectar Robbing by Bumble Bees." *PLoS ONE* 8, no. 2 (2013).

Lewis, Sara M. *Silent Sparks: The Wondrous World of Fireflies.* Princeton, NJ: Princeton University Press, 2016.

Lewis, Sara M., Choong Hay Wong, Avalon C. S. Owens, et al. "A Global Perspective on Firefly Extinction Threats." *BioScience* 70, no. 2 (2020): 157–67.

Loss, Scott R. "Understanding and Preventing Bird Collisions." Audubon Society of Central Maryland. Posted November 1, 2021. YouTube video, 1:03:47. www.youtube.com/watch?v=E8dMDFjcgr0.

Loss, Scott R., Tom Will, Sara S. Loss, and Peter P. Marra. "Bird-Building Collisions in the United States: Estimates of Annual Mortality and Species Vulnerability." *Condor* 116, no. 1 (2014): 8–23.

Machtans, Craig, Christopher Wedeles, and Erin Bayne. "A First Estimate for Canada of the Number of Birds Killed by Colliding with Building Windows." *Avian Conservation and Ecology* 8, no. 2 (2013).

Martin, Graham. *Bird Senses: How and What Birds See, Hear, Smell, Taste and Feel.* Exeter, UK: Pelagic, 2020.

Necaise, Jayme, and Tabitha Holloway. "Captive Breeding and Color Variability in the Oblong-Winged Katydid, *Amblycorypha Oblongifolia (Orthoptera: Tettigoniidae)."* Proceedings for the Invertebrates in Education and Conservation Conference, 2012.

Peng, Po, Devi Stuart-Fox, Szu-Wei Chen, et al. "High Contrast Yellow Mosaic Patterns Are Prey Attractants for Orb-Weaving Spiders." *Functional Ecology* 34, no. 4 (2020): 853–64.

Sime, Karen R. "Experimental Studies of the Host-Finding Behavior of *Trogus pennator*, a Parasitoid of Swallowtail Butterflies." *Journal of Chemical Ecology* 28, no. 7 (2002): 1377–92.

Sime, Karen R. "The Natural History of the Parasitic Wasp *Trogus Pennator* (Hymenoptera: Ichneumonidae): Host-Finding Behaviour and a Possible Host Countermeasure." *Journal of Natural History* 39, no. 17 (2005): 1367–80.

Stoddard, Mary Caswell, Harold N. Eyster, Benedict G. Hogan, Dylan H. Morris, Edward R. Soucy, and David W. Inouye. "Wild Hummingbirds Discriminate Nonspectral Colors." *Proceedings of the National Academy of Sciences* 117, no. 26 (2020): 15112–22.

Treiber, Miklos. "Composites as Host Plants and Crypts for *Synchlora aerata* (Geometridae)." *Journal of the Lepidopterists' Society* 33 (1979): 239–44.

Wang, Bo, Fangyuan Xia, Michael S. Engel, et al. "Debris-Carrying Camouflage among Diverse Lineages of Cretaceous Insects." *Science Advances* 2, no. 6 (2016).

Williams, Kathy S., and Lawrence E. Gilbert. "Insects as Selective Agents on Plant Vegetative Morphology: Egg Mimicry Reduces Egg Laying by Butterflies." *Science* 212, no. 4493 (1981): 467–69.

IMAGE CREDITS

Thank you to the following photographers
who contributed to this book.
All other photos were taken by Nancy Lawson.

Mimi Bix-Hylan	83
Richard Broughton	196
Melinda Byrd	40 bottom
Brice Claypoole	62 both, 263
Jen Cross	108, 220, 269
Judy Gallagher	26 top, 265 bottom left & bottom right
Toni Genberg	16 bottom, 72 bottom, 86, 148 top, 165, 214 bottom
Leon Grobaski	238 top
Will Heinz	11, 143 top, 282
Coy Hill	134 bottom
Ken Keefover-Ring	32 bottom, 34 top
Ric McArthur	250
Nancy E. McIntyre	243 bottom
Graham Montgomery	256 bottom
Jennifer N. Phillips	100
Andy Reago & Chrissy McClarren	176 bottom, 265 top left
Ryan Stephens	210 both
Laura Langlois Zurros	218 both